Australian BUSHRANGERS

THE ROMANCE OF ROBBERY

SACHA MOLITORISZ

Statue of Ned Kelly at Glenrowan.

Woollahra

CONTENTS

PREFACE

There was a knock on the door.

'Who is it?' I asked, wary of pay TV salesmen and market researchers. No answer. Still, like Ned Kelly, I'm a trusting soul. So, despite the silence, I opened up.

Big mistake.

I was knocked to the floor as a tall, bearded man with fiery eyes burst into my home and thrust a rusting revolver into my face.

'Bail up!' he yelled.

I was scared. Real scared. And astounded. Real astounded. A bushranger? In Sydney? In 1997?

'T-t-take anything you w-w-want,' I squeaked bravely, 'just don't shoot.'

The gunman smiled nonchalantly and returned the revolver to its holster. 'Ha,' he laughed, helping me back to my feet. 'I don't want to rob you.' He laughed some more and stroked his beard. 'No, I'm no bushranger. I'm an editor. What I want is for you to write a book for me. About bushrangers.'

I was relieved. So I agreed.

Well, maybe that isn't exactly how I came to be working on a book about bushrangers; but it is true, like most bushranging victims, that I was seemingly chosen at random. I mean, sure, I'm an experienced journalist/writer, but I have no particular expertise about bushrangers. I can't even say I've ever been mugged. Although my house was burgled once. Does that count?

On second thought, maybe I am reasonably well qualified. I have been an occasional student of history, and bushrangers, for me as for many other Australians, have always constituted one of the most romantically fascinating chapters of our history post-1788.

What's more, the deeper I delved into the subject, the more interesting it became. At each turn there was yet another remarkable tale, yet another fascinating incident. My challenge was to re-present these tales in a fresh and accessible manner. Easy in theory; not so easy in practice.

I decided to take a bushranger's approach: to don my armour and letterbox helmet, to dodge the bullets of inaccuracy and myth and to plunder the yarns of our past in order to come up with a few yarns of my own. Oh, and I wanted to do it all, as many of the original highwaymen did, with a self-imposed code of ethics and with a sense of humour and irreverence. If I managed it, I thought, the result would be both entertaining and informative.

Did I succeed? Is this book entertaining and informative?

You be the judge. If, however, after reading a few more humble pages, you find me guilty of not realising my admittedly ambitious goals, just don't be as harsh as the justices who sat in judgment over the real bushrangers. Sure, I believe in first-hand research, but I draw the line at the gallows. The death sentence? I much prefer a paragraph with a couple of puns or a sentence with a half-hearted attempt at alliteration.

Finally, I'd like to thank Bruce 'The Kid' Elder for making this modest volume possible, Robyn 'Captain Lamplight' Zwar for riding shotgun during my adventures, and Ma and Pa Molitorisz for having me, as it were.

Together, brandishing our wits, may we continue merrily on our bushranging ways for a good long while yet.

Sacha 'Captain Keyboard' Molitorisz
Sydney
November 1997

BUSHRANGERS AT BAY.
We led the hunt throughout, Ned, on the chestnut and the grey
And the troopers were three hundred yards behind,
While we emptied our sixshooters on the bushrangers at bay
In the creek, with stunted boxtree for a blind!
—Adam Lindsay Gordon

INTRODUCTION

A PRELIMINARY OVERVIEW

The history of human habitation on these islands we call Australia begins many thousands of years ago. Aborigines arrived here about 40 000 years ago, maybe long before that. From then on, for generation upon generation, the pace of life was measured, neatly following the rhythms of the land.

Violently and suddenly, change arrived in 1788 in the form of the First Fleet. Since then, the pace of life has been anything but measured. Instead, the pace of change has been frantic and unrelenting. In barely more than two hundred years, Australia has been transformed from a British colony for exiled convicts to a wealthy and independent nation with closer links to Asia and the USA than the United Kingdom.

From our vantage point late in the twentieth century, it takes a tremendous effort to imagine Australia before white occupation. Similarly, it takes a tremendous effort to imagine what it was like for those first convicts, gaolers and settlers and to comprehend their bewilderment in the face of the unknown. To the new immigrants, the Aborigines were utterly alien, the environment was hostile and unfamiliar and many of their fellow settlers (convicts and otherwise) were aggressive and dangerous.

Of course, some of the toughest new arrivals took to their new home with relish, including a number who soon seized the opportunity to escape.

Many historians identify three distinct groups of bushrangers, and these convict 'bolters' constitute the first group. ('Bolter' was a term first used in Van Diemen's Land to denote convicts who had escaped and taken to robbing settlers.) These men abandoned their shackles and fled into the bush, stealing what they could to survive. In most cases, little is known about them. These men, such as John Caesar, Matthew Brady and Jackey Jackey, were seen as an inevitable hazard of the new colonies and were usually only known in the locality

Convicts embarking for Botany Bay.

where they operated. Their exploits are contained in Chapters 1 to 3.

The second era of bushrangers coincided with the outbreak of gold fever in the 1850s, when men and mail coaches carrying large quantities of gold and cash made easy targets. Men such as Ben Hall and 'Mad' Dan Morgan became notorious, even if at first the newspapers of the day ignored bushrangers' exploits in favour of news of the latest gold strike. Only when gold fever started to recede did these outlaws begin to hog the headlines. Thanks to the invention of the telegraph, these bushrangers became known outside their locality. Even the English press reported the most sensational incidents.

By the 1850s, the nature of bushranging had changed completely from the days of the first bolters. Unlike their predecessors, many of these bushrangers were not fugitives from the law; instead many had chosen to pursue a life as a highwayman. Driven by a sense of adventure and romance, many young men aspired to enlist in the Clarke gang or with Frank Gardiner. The second era of bushranging lasted until 1872; it is covered in Chapters 4 to 9.

The third era of bushranging—bushranging's final, climactic flourish—lasted from 1878 until 1880. (Some commentators, however, such as Harry Nunn, say this third period, consisting entirely of native-born bushrangers, commences in 1861.) After 1872, there were no bushrangers until the Kelly gang captured the public's undivided attention in 1878. Again, bushranging had changed. Now it had become political. Ned Kelly and his three gang members came to symbolise the hatred and distrust many poor Australians felt towards the police. Authorities at the time were genuinely concerned that Ned and his devoted sympathisers might provoke a violent popular uprising in northern Victoria. In Australia and back in England, the public was fascinated and more inches of newspaper space were devoted to the Kelly gang than to all the previous bushrangers combined. This makes the history of the Kellys relatively easy to reconstruct. Chapter 10 is devoted to Captain Moonlite and, among other things, his exploits of 1879; Chapters 11 and 12 are devoted to the Kellys.

So, there were three distinct eras, but a number of factors linked the very first bushranger to the very last. One such factor was youth. Most bushrangers, not surprisingly, died a violent death, either by gun or by noose, and most were very young when they died. Some were in their teens, most were in their twenties. Ben Hall was shot dead at twenty-seven; Ned Kelly was hanged at twenty-five; and, at thirty-four, Captain Thunderbolt was a veritable senior citizen of bushranging when he was shot dead. Careers were generally brief (Thunderbolt's, lasting seven years, was probably the longest) and only a few bushrangers survived beyond their bushranging years.

Another linking factor was a self-imposed code of ethics. From Matthew Brady in Tasmania in the 1820s to Ben Hall in New South Wales in the 1850s to Ned Kelly in Victoria in 1880, many bushrangers were polite, especially to women. Many preferred not to use violence and some even returned property to victims they thought were poor. Sure, there were plenty of bushrangers who would slit your throat for a penny without a second thought, men such as Michael Howe and 'Mad' Dan Morgan, but these days bushrangers, on the whole, are remembered for their chivalry.

Which brings us to the 'bushranger legend', of which chivalry is an integral part. Bushrangers nowadays are perceived as romantic, daring and brave. It was not always so. Back when they were terrifying travellers and holding up homesteads, most bushrangers

Sydney Town, just a few years after the arrival of the First Fleet.

were considered rough, dangerous and bad. Sure, they had their fans, but there were more detractors.

How is it that over the years they have nearly all been turned into heroes? This is partly a function of time—the past always looks more romantic and less dangerous than it actually was. As well, Australians have a fascination with their criminal past and an affinity for the underdog who found himself battling authority to survive. The bushranger legend is also a function of how the facts have been passed on. Since many of the relevant incidents, particularly in the early years, were only recorded orally, there was always room for a little embellishment. It is impossible to know whether several significant incidents, such as Captain Thunderbolt returning the money he stole from a German band with interest (see Chapter 8), is myth or fact. It is important to remember that many of the bushrangers had devoted sympathisers and that these were the people most likely to note down the bushrangers' stories.

Accounts of the bushrangers differ markedly. For instance, when Thunderbolt was shot dead, some accounts say his gun was loaded, others say it wasn't. The discrepancies extend to crucial dates and often the variations are huge; some reports say Frank Gardiner died in 1883, others say he survived until 1903. Then, of course, there's the matter of spelling. Was it Alexander Pierce or Pearce? Williams or

Williamson? One hundred-and-fifty years ago, literacy was at a much lower level than it is today. As a result, the task of compiling a definitive, infallible history of the bushrangers is difficult, if not impossible.

While we're on the subject of disclaimers, this volume does not seek to be a comprehensive account of every Australian bushranger (it is estimated there were, in total, between 350 and 450 of them). Instead, it concentrates on some of the more interesting and intriguing characters. By choosing bushrangers from each of the three eras and from across various States, hopefully a bigger picture emerges.

Finally, a word about the words themselves. 'Bolter' has already been explained, and the word 'bushranger' is addressed in Chapter 1, but a few other terms bear explaining. 'Bail up!', a phrase used when stopping and robbing travellers, was current in the 1840s. This was what most bushrangers first yelled at their victims. Meanwhile, 'stick up', brought into popular use by the bushrangers, had a wider meaning, that is, to rob.

With that, cast your mind back to a world without television, a world without Pepsi, a world without cars. Cast your mind back to 1788, when Sydney Harbour looked like a pretty fine place to pitch camp and as good a place as any to make a home for several hundred convicts …

CHAPTER 1

THE FIRST RECORDED BUSHRANGER

Who was the first Australian bushranger?

That's a tough question. Much easier to answer is the silly-sounding question: When was the first bushranger? The answer being—probably about two minutes after the First Fleet dropped anchor at Sydney Town back in January 1788.

Try to picture the scene. Two years ago, back on the mean streets of East London, you stole a sack of spuds to feed your family. The police caught you and, once tried and found guilty, you were

sentenced to a lengthy prison term. Then, after a few months shut in an overcrowded British prison, you suddenly find yourself crammed inside the smelly bowels of a big sailing ship. Yep, you're aboard one of the eleven ships of the First Fleet, bound for a fledgling penal colony called Australia, situated somewhere on the other side of the planet.

After a gruelling, exhausting journey, you reach your destination. It is, essentially, a prison without bars and it is thoroughly unfamiliar.

Convicts being taken to ships bound for New Holland.

between Sydney and its nearest neighbours. Among your convict friends, literacy levels and geographical knowledge are extremely poor. It isn't known exactly how many of the dead runaways perished in the vain attempt at reaching another settlement.

The men who eventually become known as bushrangers, however, have no illusions of reaching Singapore or Hong Kong. The first such man to be recorded by name is John Caesar, also known as Black Caesar, a 'Negro' who, like you, arrived at Sydney as a convict on the First Fleet. He has been described as the 'hardest working man in the colony … but in his intellects he did not very widely differ from a brute.' In June 1789, the tall, muscular convict takes to the bush with a soldier's musket and ammunition. The fugitive starts prowling around the fringes of the colony, stealing enough food to survive, but he is quickly recaptured by another convict, William Saltmarsh.

Caesar soon escapes again, this time in an Aboriginal canoe and this time carrying food and an iron pot as well as a gun and ammunition. He heads to Rose Hill (Parramatta), where he stays with a native tribe until he 'offends them'. Wounded by spears, the giant convict staggers into town to surrender, whereupon he is transported to Norfolk Island, the settlement to which the most difficult re-offenders are sent. After four years at Norfolk, Caesar returns to New South Wales in July 1794. Once again he takes to the bush. Once more he is captured and once more he escapes.

This time Caesar becomes the leader of a gang of like-minded 'bolters', plundering what they can from travellers and homesteads. Growing frustrated, the authorities declare him an outlaw, offering a reward of five gallons of rum for any man who can capture or kill him. Eager to claim the rum, a man named Winbow tracks the escaped convict to his hideout near present-day Concord, where before dawn he shoots him. 'He had given more trouble than any other convict in the settlement,' writes Tasmanian Lieutenant-Governor David Collins after Caesar has died from his wound.

Details of the lives of these early bolters are hard to come by, primarily because their exploits usually aren't recorded. As a result, many of the exciting deeds and violent crimes of these men are quickly forgotten, but soon a word appears to describe this new breed of highwayman. The word is 'bushranger' and it is used at least as early as 1805, when the *Sydney Gazette* reports that a cart had been stopped by men 'whose appearance sanctioned the suspicion of their being bushrangers.'

For the next seventy-five years, it is a word Australians are going to hear often.

You are terrified. In the first ten months after the First Fleet arrives, fifty-five of the 1124 arrivals have died of sickness, four have been killed by natives and five have been hanged. Despite the unknown dangers of an alien environment, there is a powerful temptation to risk it all and head for the bush, stealing what you need to survive. Indeed, during those first ten months, fourteen men have died after succumbing to that temptation. That's the number of men presumed dead after going missing in the bush.

Of course, not all these fugitives are what you'd call highwaymen. Some merely want to escape. These men, hearing of settlements at places such as Singapore and Hong Kong, strike out north or west, not knowing the tremendous expanse of land and ocean that lies

CHAPTER 2

THE CONVICT CANNIBAL

ALEXANDER PEARCE

These days, the ruggedly beautiful island of Tasmania is sleepy and scenic. Two hundred years ago, however, Van Diemen's Land was a brutal open-air prison for the toughest and meanest of criminals.

Life for the early convicts and their captors was harsh everywhere in Australia, but nowhere was it more harsh than in Van Diemen's Land, settled by Europeans in 1803. (Life became even more harsh for the nine tribes of Aborigines who, after 30 000 years on the island, were soon methodically exterminated.) The worst prisoners in England were sent to Australia; the worst prisoners in Australia were sent to Van Diemen's Land.

During the settlement's early years, convicts made up about half of the island's population. While many of these prisoners found it easy enough to escape into the bush, the problem was, once they'd escaped, how could they survive? Some, such as Alexander Pearce, resorted to the most drastic measures imaginable.

Soon after the disciplinarian William Sorell became Lieutenant-Governor in 1817, he devised a tough way to punish badly-behaved convicts and recaptured escapees: he sent them into exile on Sarah Island. As on the mainland of Australia, most of the population of Van Diemen's Land lived on the east coast, most commonly in

Hobart Town. Way over on the other side of the island, where the Gordon and Franklin rivers are part of what remains one of the world's most pristine and precious landscapes, Sarah Island was turned into a penal settlement. Here recalcitrant convicts could be sent to log huon pine for shipbuilding.

The convicts who arrived here must have felt they'd reached the end of the earth. The Deputy Surveyor of the day described Sarah Island as 'so completely shut in by the surrounding rugged, closely wooded and altogether impractical country, that escape by land is next to impossible.' Escape by sea was equally difficult. Sarah Island, perched in the middle of Macquarie Harbour, is more than 300 kilometres from Hobart by boat. Even in good weather, the journey took two weeks. As a final insult, the mouth of Macquarie Harbour, aptly dubbed Hell's Gates, was treacherously narrow.

On 23 January 1822, the first 110 settlers, half of them convicts, arrived from Hobart. As usual, some of the more optimistic convicts immediately tried to escape. In March, two of these bolted from a work gang. A week later six more fled. A search party of two soldiers and three convicts set off in pursuit. Thanks to the wilderness, not one of the thirteen men was ever seen again.

Six months later, in September, after a long, freezing winter, Irishman Alexander Pearce was among the second wave of convicts to arrive at Sarah Island. Sent to Hobart for seven years for stealing shoes, Pearce was sent to the west coast for 'divers misdemeanours', including forgery. A month after he had passed through Hell's Gates, Pearce fled into the bush with seven others, each man carrying stolen provisions on his back.

As the days passed, chilling rain and biting cold took their toll. The men were only travelling about 4 kilometres per day and each day the outlook deteriorated. Day eight: suddenly, three of the party had vanished, apparently hoping to make it back to Sarah Island. Day twelve: the party reached a river; two men couldn't swim, so the others dragged them across on logs. Day fifteen: another river but this time the men were too weak to drag each other across.

The five remaining men were exhausted and starving. Unable to find food in the hostile environment, their talk turned to cannibalism. Could they? There was no choice. The men knew too little about this environment to catch any wildlife or know which plants or shrubs could be eaten. Soon they were drawing straws. Thomas Bodenham drew the short one. He was kneeling down to pray when he was felled by a blow to the head. The date was 5 October.

For a few days, Bodenham's remains sustained the remaining four fugitives, who had by now divided into two camps: Pearce and 22-year-old former baker John Mather against two former partners-in-crime, Robert Greenhill and Matthew Travis. After a week had passed, the four were hungry again. Mather foraged for roots, boiling them up in a tin pot but they made him violently sick. Sensing an opportunity, Greenhill crept up with an axe, swinging down hard at Mather's head. At that very moment, Mather moved and the axe glanced off the side of his head. The two struggled and Mather snatched the axe from his attacker's grasp.

Mather's good fortune didn't last. It wasn't long before Pearce proved himself a fickle friend, ganging up with Greenhill and Travis against the increasingly agitated baker. The three men leapt on Mather and killed him. The men feasted, but already Pearce was worried, knowing how tight the other two were. He was particularly worried about Greenhill, who had been the executioner of both Bodenham and Mather.

Fortunately for Pearce, however, four days after Mather became lunch, Travis was bitten by a snake. Travis wanted to die in peace and Greenhill promised he would never betray him. Travis could hardly walk but Greenhill promised he would never abandon his mate. Days

The tough disciplinarian William Sorell became Lieutenant-Governor of Van Diemen's Land in April 1817.

dragged on as the three men ate the last of Mather's remains. Six days after Travis was bitten, the men decided to start walking again. Greenhill half-carried Travis and, knowing what a burden he was being, Travis was nervous. Would he be the next victim?

That night, around the campfire, Travis fell asleep. He woke with a start, terrified to see Pearce and Greenhill huddling together and whispering. Greenhill calmed his mate, who soon fell asleep again. Travis was killed minutes later.

And then there were two. For a couple of days, Pearce and Greenhill stuffed themselves, pledging not to betray each other. By this stage, their clothes had been torn from their bodies and their feet were bare but they were elated when they reached a plain. Were they near a settlement? Eventually, the men sighted a plume of smoke. As they advanced, they realised they had stumbled upon about fifty Aborigines. Armed with a stick and an axe, Pearce and Greenhill screamed and hollered as they ran into the camp, frightening off the tribe. The two men gleefully ate the kangaroo and possum flesh that had been left behind. The next day Pearce and Greenhill came upon a smaller group of Aborigines and did exactly the same thing.

Sure, they had pledged eternal brotherhood, but the relationship between the two men soon soured. Greenhill carried the axe, and Pearce didn't trust him. In the middle of the night of 6 November, six weeks after escaping, Pearce noticed that Greenhill was in a deep sleep. Heart pumping furiously, Pearce crept over to Greenhill, snatched the axe from under Greenhill's makeshift pillow and, before his victim could move, brought it down on his head. Greenhill died instantly. This time, Pearce didn't eat the remains, leaving them untouched.

A week later, Pearce bumped into a flock of sheep. He was exhausted but his heart leapt. He had made it! He had crossed over to the fringes of the settled east coast. His first concern, however, was his stomach. He tackled a sheep but was so weak it dragged him along the ground before escaping. Finally he managed to catch a lamb. While he was tucking into the raw flesh, Pearce was startled by a voice threatening to shoot him. Pearce turned and was startled to recognise the man behind the musket. Little is known of the man, but he and Pearce may have worked together stealing sheep. The man took Pearce to his hut and nursed him for eleven days.

One night, while Pearce's saviour made a trip to Hobart, two men carrying muskets and knapsacks appeared at the hut. They were sheep

Hobart Town, on the River Derwent, Van Diemen's Land.

thieves Ralph Churton and William Davis, who persuaded Pearce to join them. He did, but the gang of bushrangers was not particularly successful. On 11 January 1823, the three men were surprised and captured by a group of soldiers. On 14 April, Churton and Davis were executed. Pearce, however, though he confessed to killing and eating his co-escapees, was simply shipped back to Macquarie Harbour. Perhaps no-one believed his remarkable story.

Pearce wasn't about to quietly pass the rest of his days at Macquarie Harbour, however. On 16 November 1823, after spending nine months in chains, Pearce escaped again, this time with a former farm labourer from Shropshire, Thomas Cox. Pearce had no intention of heading east again; this time he struck out north, towards Port Dalrymple. They didn't make it far, for when they reached a river, Cox admitted he couldn't swim. Pearce was livid. As Cox knelt down to build a campfire, he was struck on the head. Pearce was back to his

old ways, killing and eating his companion.

He had changed, though. Pearce no longer had the stomach to live this way. On 21 November, while navigating Macquarie Harbour, the crew of the *Waterloo* saw smoke. They approached the shore and found Pearce, who told them Cox had drowned. Pearce was handcuffed, but a piece of human flesh was found in his pocket. 'Tell me, Pearce, did you do the deed?' asked Lieutenant Cuthbertson. 'Yes,' said Pearce, 'and I am willing to die for it.' The next day Pearce led a party to the remains of Thomas Cox. Pearce said later that he had surrendered because, after murdering Cox, he had become weary of life and was willing to die for his crimes.

On 20 June 1824, Pearce was tried in the new Supreme Court at Hobart. Chief Justice John Pedder was a relatively humane and lenient man, but here he was faced with a case 'too inhuman to comment upon.' Alexander Pearce was hanged on 19 July 1824.

CHAPTER 3

VAN DIEMEN'S LAND BOLTERS

MICHAEL HOWE • MATTHEW BRADY MARTIN CASH

Alexander Pearce was by no means the only bushranger in Tasmania's history. Although Pearce's exploits are the most implausible and dramatic of any Van Diemen's Land bolter, his bushranging career was unsuccessful and brief. Other southern fugitives did far better out of raiding homesteads and stalking the highways and byways. Some, such as Martin Cash, even lived to tell the tale in the local pub.

One man with an unusually long bushranging career was Michael Howe, a convict who was busily bushranging well before Alexander Pearce even arrived in Van Diemen's Land. Howe was born in Yorkshire in 1787. Twenty-four years later he was sentenced to seven years' transportation for highway robbery. He reached Hobart Town

on 4 June 1812, where he was put to work for a grazier and merchant, but promptly escaped. Howe teamed up with a gang of runaways led by another escapee, a tough guy named James Whitehead. On 28 May 1814, concerned at the escalation of lawlessness, Governor Macquarie offered an amnesty for any crime short of murder to convict bolters who surrendered before the end of the year. Howe and Whitehead were among those who happily took advantage of the offer and returned to Hobart, but only long enough to catch up with friends and eat well before bolting once more.

The Howe/Whitehead gang went to work, methodically plundering homesteads at New Norfolk, 50 kilometres from Hobart.

They were dangerous and anarchic times during which the bushrangers stole whatever they could and set fire to barns and wheatstacks belonging to Hobart's police magistrate. At this stage, the total population of Van Diemen's Land was only about 2000. On 10 March 1815, a party of five irate settlers took off after the gang, but the gang took cover and opened fire. Two settlers were killed and three others were badly wounded.

After a second destructive raid on the police magistrate's property, the situation had become so bad that the Lieutenant-Governor declared a state of martial law on 11 May 1815. (Though illegal—the permission of the Governor had not been obtained—martial law remained in force for six months.) A few days later, the gang was surprised by the 46th Regiment, who shot and killed Whitehead. Howe and Whitehead had a deal: if one of them was killed, the other would decapitate him, so no-one could claim the reward. Howe did as he had agreed. The head was found two years later. In the meantime, Howe was the gang's new leader.

At its peak, the gang boasted twenty-eight members, each of them kept in line with a kind of military discipline. But, after two more of his gang were killed in March 1817, Howe thought he might do better alone. Well, almost alone, he took his Aboriginal mistress, Mary Cockerill, alias Black Mary, with him. A month later, the incompetent and profligate Lieutenant-Governor Davey was replaced by William Sorell, the efficient military man who later decided to create a penal settlement at Macquarie Harbour. Sorell was eager to capture Michael Howe, who by now had a reputation as the 'worst of the bushrangers'.

On 9 April, the same day Sorell arrived in Hobart, a military patrol stumbled on Howe and Black Mary. Both started running, but Black Mary, being pregnant, couldn't keep up. Howe turned to fire at the soldiers and hit Black Mary instead. (In fact, it's unclear whether he deliberately aimed at her.) She fell, wounded; Howe escaped into the bush. Black Mary was so unimpressed that she went on to give the soldiers enough information to track down a number of Howe's former gang members.

Two weeks later, Howe, the self-proclaimed 'Governor of the Ranges', sent a letter to the 'Governor of the Town', William Sorell. Howe said he would surrender and give information about the remainder of his gang if he was granted a pardon in return. Sorell, still struggling to supress lawlessness, welcomed the offer. After Howe ambled into Hobart under escort on 29 April, he talked and talked. Much of his information was useless, but he did cause a stir by implicating the Reverend Robert Knopwood in the bushrangers' activities. Governor Macquarie wasn't impressed, asking Sorell to exercise 'forbearance and delicacy'. In other words, the matter was swept under the rug.

While Howe was in loose custody in Hobart, the new chief of the gang, Geary, was shot dead. On 28 July 1817, Howe fled into the bush again, but by now the Government really did have the upper hand. After some were killed and others surrendered, Howe and George Watts were the only members of the gang still at large. They were operating separately and Watts decided he might be able to win both a reward and a pardon by helping to capture Howe.

Watts sought out an associate of Howe, William Drewe, and together the pair set a trap for Howe. It worked, and soon Howe's wrists were bound and he was being led to Hobart. On the way, however, Howe managed to free his wrists. He pulled out a dagger he'd hidden in his clothing and stabbed Watts in the back. Almost at the same time, he grabbed Watts' gun, spun around and shot Drewe through the head. Howe escaped; Watts died a few days later.

The worst of the bushrangers was still at large. Lieutenant-Governor Sorell decided to offer a full pardon and passage back to England for any prisoner who helped capture Howe. Because he worked alone, he was difficult to betray. When he was hungry, he simply appeared at a hut demanding food and am-munition. Most of his victims weren't about to argue.

One afternoon, deep in the hinterland, Howe was startled to see a soldier ahead of him. Instinctively, the bush-ranger dropped his knap-sack and fled. Inside was a book made of kangaroo skin in which Howe had jotted his thoughts in kangaroo blood. The journal revealed Howe's loneliness. He dreamed of being murdered by Aborigines and of growing fruits and vegetables for himself. After years in the bush, he was looking very much the wild man of the woods in the clothes he had cut from kangaroo skins and his long black beard.

If he had completely avoided human contact, he might have died of old age, but Howe occasionally met with a kangaroo hunter called Warburton. In October 1818, it was Warburton who decided to betray the final member of Whitehead's gang. With two others, Warburton set an ambush, but before he could be captured, Howe managed to turn and flee into the forest. His three pursuers were close behind. Howe stumbled and, when he stood up, was shot in the chest. The bushranger pulled out a dagger but was unable to use it before one of the men had smashed him over the head with the butt of a gun. It was 21 October 1818, and Michael Howe was finally dead.

In 1822, four years after Howe died, Alexander Pearce arrived at Sarah Island. In June 1824, an articulate forger named Matthew Brady arrived at Macquarie Harbour, just in time to hear about the hanging of Alexander Pearce.

Howe and Pearce were both dangerous, violent men; Matthew Brady, by contrast, steered away from violence and had a reputation for treating women well. As soon as he arrived in Hobart in late 1820, he made several escape attempts, which is how he came to find himself on Sarah Island. It was from there, on 9 June 1824, that Brady and twelve other convicts escaped in a frail boat. Unlike Pearce two years earlier, they decided their best chance was not overland, but the 320 kilometre trip around the southern edge of the island. Somehow, the men successfully navigated their way through the narrow mouth of Macquarie Harbour, dodged the musket balls of pursuers and, nine days later, washed up near the mouth of the Derwent River.

With little other choice, the men turned to bushranging and Brady soon established himself as the gang's leader. Late on 25 October 1824, Brady and an accomplice burst into the hut of Thomas Kenton, a former convict who was in league with the

The Derwent River at New Norfolk.

Martin Cash, one of the few bushrangers to die in his own bed.

bushrangers. This time, however, Kenton had betrayed them—he was waiting for Brady with armed soldiers. Brady's accomplice fled; Brady himself was captured. With the soldiers gone for reinforcements and Kenton outside fetching water, Brady held his wrists in the fire, gritting his teeth against the pain, until the rope broke. When Kenton returned, Brady aimed a gun at his head. Kenton begged for mercy and Brady granted it, before fleeing into the night.

(More than a year later, in March 1826, Brady committed his only act of deliberate murder: visiting Kenton at a small-town inn and shooting him dead.)

Just like his predecessors, George Arthur, the new Lieutenant-Governor of the colony, was having trouble enforcing law and order. In April 1825, Brady pinned a note on the door of the Royal Oak Inn:

> It has caused Matthew Brady much concern that such a person as Sir George Arthur is at large. Twenty gallons of rum will be given to any person who will deliver this person unto me.

Arthur was irritated by the note, but he was more irritated by the gang's successes, so he agreed to let a tough Irish convict named Cowan join the gang as a spy. In return, Cowan would receive a pardon and a passage home. In late March 1826, the gang of ten was ambushed at their mountain hideout in the island's north-east by a party of soldiers. The gang scattered and Brady and a mate ran along a river. When Brady was shot in the leg, the pair leapt into the current.

John Batman was a prominent landholder in the region, the man who, ten years later, co-founded Melbourne. Hearing Brady's gang was nearby, Batman set off in pursuit. He soon tracked down a man limping through the trees. 'Are you a soldier?' asked Brady, reaching for his gun. 'I am no soldier, Brady,' came the reply. 'I am John Batman. Surrender, for there is no chance for you.' Brady surrendered. His trial began in Hobart on 25 April. Despite petitions and protests, particularly from adoring women, Brady was hanged on 4 May 1826.

'A bushranger's life is wretched and miserable,' he said while awaiting the noose. 'There is no peace, day or night.'

'Why did you not give yourself up then?'

'Because I always knew it would end this way and I wanted to live as long as I could.'

After Brady's gang was shattered, Van Diemen's Land enjoyed relative peace until Britton's gang

John Batman.

arrived to terrorise the northern settlements in 1832 and 1833. Then, in the 1840s, Martin Cash was the final flourish for Tasmanian bushranging. Cash landed at Sydney in 1828 and was immediately sent to work in New South Wales' Hunter Valley, where he was granted his freedom in 1834. In 1837, after having been accused of cattle stealing, he fled to Hobart with his love, Bessie Clifford, the wife of a British army officer.

Over the next few years, Cash earned a living in a variety of jobs. While the couple were living at Campbell Town, a man named Miller asked for a night's lodging. Suddenly, the police were at the door. Miller fled, leaving his swag; the police searched it, found it full of pilfered property and arrested Martin Cash. At Launceston on 24 March 1840, Cash was convicted of possessing stolen goods. After escaping from a work gang, he was recaptured and sent to Port Arthur, where the prison was reputed to be cruel and escape-proof. Cash, however, escaped by swimming from the peninsula to the mainland, but after five days he was recaptured.

Cash pondered how to escape. On Boxing Day 1842, he and two others—Lawrence Kavanagh (who had been sent to Port Arthur after bushranging in Sydney's Rose Bay) and George Jones—fled into the bush. Several days later, after swimming across the bay and crawling past a sentry box, they were free. After sticking up numerous homesteads, the three men stumbled on the perfect career (bushranging) and the perfect hideout (a cave atop Mount Drome-dary, 24 kilometres from Hobart).

At the base of Mount Dromedary lived a family who knew Cash. The three convicts rested there while the wife travelled to Hobart and brought back Bessie, reuniting her with her man. The men, who came to be known as Cash & Co, took to raiding homesteads, but garnered a reputation for civility and non-violence. On 22 February 1843, they plundered jewellery, wine and dresses (for Bessie) from the Shone property near New Norfolk.

When Bessie was taken prisoner in March 1843, for possessing stolen goods, Cash responded as Matthew Brady might have. He sent a letter to Lieutenant-Governor John Franklin:

> Messrs Cash & Co beg to notify His Excellency Sir John Franklin that a very respectable person named Mrs Cash is now falsely imprisoned in Hobart Town, and if the said Mrs Cash is not released forthwith and properly remunerated, we will, in the first instance, visit Government House and beginning with Sir John, administer a wholesome lesson in the shape of a sound flogging; after which we will pay the same currency to all his followers.

Bessie was released on 28 April—it had nothing to do with the note, the police hoped that she would lead them to Cash & Co.

On 3 July, the gang committed its first highway robbery, bailing up the Launceston passenger coach. It was the same day that two Aboriginal blacktrackers arrived in Hobart; they were soon on the bushrangers' trail. Things weren't going too well for the gang: a week later, Lawrence Kavanagh's gun exploded. His arm was shattered and he was losing blood. He decided to surrender.

Bessie, meanwhile, had not returned from Hobart. Rumours were spreading that she had taken up with a man there. Spurred on by jealousy, Cash became dangerously reckless, travelling to the colony's capital to confront Bessie himself. Before he had found her, however, he was recognised and soon a gaggle of pursuers was chasing him through the streets. Outside the Old Commodore Inn, Constable Peter Winstanley lunged at Cash, but the bushranger shot him dead. Cash managed to fire one more shot (shattering one man's nose) before he was knocked unconscious and captured.

Cash and Kavanagh were both sentenced to death but, two days before they were due to be hanged, both were told there had been a stay of execution. Kavanagh was transported to Norfolk Island, which had been recolonised in 1825 after lying abandoned for nineteen years. Cash was kept in his Hobart cell for fifteen months, then sent to Norfolk Island as well. George Jones was less fortunate. Six months after his co-escapees were taken prisoner, Jones was hanged at Hobart Town gaol.

For Kavanagh and Cash, the story was not over yet. Norfolk Island, home to 2000 convicts, was intended to be 'a place of extremist punishment short of death.' Conditions were harsh and it took only a minor incident—a group of constables confiscating the prisoners' billies—to trigger a mutiny by twenty men, led by William Westwood, alias Jackey Jackey, who had been a bushranger in New South Wales. On an early morning rampage, Jackey Jackey killed four prison officers. When order was restored, twenty-six men were charged with murder. Although he had only played a small part, Lawrence Kavanagh was one of them.

On 18 July 1846, a new commandant name John Price arrived at Norfolk Island to enforce a heavy-handed discipline. After exchanging an emotional goodbye with Cash, Kavanagh was one of twelve men hanged on 13 October. Under the new commandant, conditions deteriorated so much that reports of the floggings and insanity at Norfolk Island ultimately convinced English authorities to overhaul the entire convict system. In January 1853, John Price left Norfolk Island (to become chief of the Victorian prison system). Cash stayed on the island.

On 14 May 1854, Cash married an Irish ticket-of-leave convict, Mary Bennett. In September, Cash received his ticket-of-leave, and the pair immediately left for Hobart. In 1855, the couple had a son; the following year the family left for New Zealand, where they stayed for four years. On their return, they bought a property at Glenorchy, near Hobart, abundant with apple trees.

When Martin Cash finally died in August 1877, aged sixty-nine, he had not only lived through exciting escapades, terrifying escapes and inhuman prisons, he had seen Van Diemen's Land changed utterly. From its beginnings as a home for the toughest convicts, it was gradually turning into the Apple Isle. Having changed from bushranger into apple farmer, the life of Martin Cash neatly symbolised Tasmania's transformation.

Convicts working in the harsh penal colony of Norfolk Island.

CHAPTER 4

FROM BUSHRANGING TO BARKEEPING
OR ... FROM DUFFING HORSES TO PULLING BEERS

'GENERAL' FRANK GARDINER

Most bushrangers were dead before they reached thirty. Frank Gardiner, after successfully pulling off the biggest robbery in bushranging history, after cheating death time after time, after inspiring countless youths to pursue a life of crime, ended up a barman in the United States.

The man who called himself the Prince of Tobymen (toby is an old English word for highway) came to Australia in 1831 from Great Britain and lived between Goulburn and the place which later became Canberra. Twenty years later he was in Melbourne's Pentridge prison for stealing thirty-two horses, but after serving only five months of a three-year sentence he escaped by overpowering a guard. He returned to the Goulburn region and in 1854 he was sentenced to seven years on Cockatoo Island, again for horse-stealing.

On his release in December 1859 Gardiner travelled to the Burrangong goldfields (near present-day Young) where he opened a butcher's shop with William Fogg. Some said that nearly all the meat in Gardiner's shop was 'on the cross' (that is, stolen), so it wasn't such a surprise when he was finally arrested for selling stolen beef. Granted bail, Gardiner decided he'd spent enough of his life behind bars, so he became a fully-fledged highwayman, teaming up with another bushranger, John Piesley. He started robbing and plundering almost immediately and, through his daring escapes, narrow scrapes and thrilling exploits, managed to become quite popular.

But not with the police. On 16 July 1861, Sergeant John Middleton and Trooper William Hosie of Tuena had a suspicion they would find Gardiner at the farm of his former business partner, William Fogg. When they arrived, Hosie waited outside, while Middleton knocked and was invited in. There Middleton saw the Fogg family and an old man who worked as a dairyman. No sign of Gardiner though in the single-room slab hut divided at one end by a calico screen.

Suddenly Middleton noticed a movement behind the screen. He walked up to it. Then, a voice said, 'Stand back or I'll shoot.' Middleton, pistol in hand, pulled back the screen. Sure enough, there was Gardiner, holding a revolver. Both men fired. Middleton's heavy ball hit Gardiner in the head, but improbably glanced off his forehead. The bushranger was not seriously injured, but his face was covered in powder burns. Gardiner's shot hit Middleton in the mouth. Before the trooper could reload, Gardiner fired again, hitting Middleton in the left hand and leg.

Middleton staggered from the hut. 'Don't attempt to come in here,' Gardiner yelled after him. Hosie ignored the warning and entered; suddenly he and the outlaw were face to face. Again, both men fired. Hosie missed, Gardiner hit. Hosie was struck in the head. He fell. Middleton stumbled back in, this time brandishing a leaded whip (a whip with a heavy handle that could be used as a truncheon). Middleton struck Gardiner on the head with it.

Hosie struggled back to his feet and leapt at the bushranger while Middleton kept hitting him in the face. Inevitably, the two police overpowered Gardiner, who finally collapsed. Still, Middleton was impressed. 'Well, Gardiner, you are the gamest man I ever fell in with,' he said, slipping on the handcuffs.

A brief bushranging career might have come to an end then and there, except that Middleton was dealing with 'Darkie' Gardiner, the Houdini of the bush. Middleton decided to ride to Bigga for help, telling Hosie to guard the outlaw. Soon after Middleton left, however, Gardiner lunged at Hosie and the pair wrestled and traded punches on the floor of Fogg's hut. They fought right out the door and into the yard, where Gardiner, still handcuffed, broke free and made a dash for the river. Hosie fired his pistol, but missed. Gardiner grabbed a stick and lunged and the two fought again until they collapsed. When Gardiner regained consciousness, Hosie had the pistol pointed at him.

After several hours, Hosie decided Middleton must have died from his wounds on the way back to Bigga, so he started out to take his prisoner to Bigga himself. Bad move: Hosie, Gardiner and Fogg

Frank Gardiner, the lovable rogue who, like Ben Hall, attained folk hero status.

hadn't gone far when they were stopped by two bushrangers, one being Gardiner's partner, John Piesley. Hosie said later he would have been killed, except that Fogg pleaded for the bushrangers to spare the policeman's life. They did so. They also, of course, freed Gardiner.

That was Hosie's story; John Piesley gave a different account. Piesley claimed Fogg had paid Hosie £50 to release the prisoner. Either way, Hosie made it back to Bigga late in the afternoon, weak and exhausted. Middleton had fared even worse: he had lost his way and fallen unconscious. Feverish and near death, he arrived in Bigga in the evening. He did, however, make a full recovery and in 1875 he was awarded a silver medal for his 'Gallant and Faithfull Service' during the incident at Fogg's.

About six months later, in February 1862, Piesley was captured and charged with the murder of an innkeeper near Bigga. He was hanged at Bathurst Gaol that same month.

Gardiner, meanwhile, was on the loose and on a spree, making sure he had fun as he went. In April, at Crowther station, Gardiner and some bushranging mates not only stuck up all hands, but one of his gang played the piano while the others danced. At Crookes station one played concertina and another sang.

All the while, Gardiner was mindful of his image. A letter appeared in the *Lachlan Miner* of 19 April 1862:

Sir, having seen a paragraph in one of the papers, wherein it is said that I took the boots off a man's feet, and that I also took the last few shillings that another man had, I wish it to be made known that I did not do anything of the kind. The man who took the boots was in my company, and for so doing I discharged him the following day. Silver I never took from a man yet, and the shot that was fired at the sticking-up of Messrs Horsington and Hewitt was by accident, and the man who did it I also discharged. As for

Sir Frederick Pottinger, Inspector of Police.

a mean, low, or petty action, I never committed it in my life… Fearing nothing, I remain, Prince of Tobymen, Francis Gardner [sic], the Highwayman.'

Gardiner obviously considered himself a man of honour. It was said that during his exploits he carried with him a tattered volume of the poetry of romantic poet Lord Byron. Gardiner probably considered himself one of Byron's 'noble pirates'.

He certainly had a good deal of sympathy. As one concerned Carcoar local wrote, 'I believe there is scarcely a house between Mount Macquarie and the Abercrombie River that will not afford any criminal shelter when required. I am satisfied that there are hundreds of lads in the neighbourhood under twenty that would give one of their eyes to have the same notoriety as Gilbert and Gardiner … Something must be done by the Government or things will become worse and worse and what will be the end of it no one can tell.'

Almost each day a new robbery was reported in the Burrangong/Cowra/Forbes area, until the momentous haul of 15 June 1862. The target was the Forbes Gold Escort, a covered mail coach drawn by four horses making its weekly trip to Orange. On board were four iron boxes packed with gold and cash. As well as the driver, John Fegan, four policemen were on guard aboard the coach.

Fifty-six kilometres out from Forbes, on a curve near a landmark known as the Eugowra Rocks, the coach came across a bullock team blocking its path. 'Bail up!' yelled a bushranger with a blackened face. As the police were raising their rifles, Gardiner yelled: 'Fire!'

Lead showered the coach and two of the officers were struck. One of the bullets knocked John Fegan's hat from his head. A second round of shots forced the troopers to leap from the coach. The horses reared and the coach tumbled onto its side. The police and driver fled; the bushrangers seized the loot. they counted it up—£14 000. Not bad considering that in 1862 a policeman earned about £60 in a year. The gang retired to Wheogo Mountain to camp for the night, where they divided up their takings.

The police were soon out in force and a party of police recovered more than half the gold from a packhorse which broke away from members of the gang during a wild chase through the bush. No more of the stolen property was ever recovered, but about a dozen suspects were tracked down and arrested. One was Daniel Charters, who turned informer, telling police that Gardiner had led the robbery. Based on Charters' evidence, Henry Manns was hanged and Alexander Fordyce and John Bow were sentenced to life in prison. Both were released after eleven years. For his help, Charters was acquitted and given a job breaking horses for the police service.

But the mastermind behind the biggest robbery in bushranging history was still on the run, and Sir Frederick Pottinger, the unpopular man in charge of the western district police, was determined to apprehend him. Knowing Gardiner had fallen in love with Kate Brown (whose husband had been arrested as another suspect in the Escort gold robbery), Pottinger and eight of his men hid themselves near the Brown house in the middle of one dark night. The police waited. Hours later, a man stepped out of Kate Brown's home, mounted his white horse and rode towards Pottinger.

Right in front of Pottinger, the white horse stopped. It was definitely Gardiner. Pottinger aimed his gun at the bushranger and told him to surrender. The policeman pulled the trigger, but his gun misfired. Gardiner's horse bolted. 'Shoot the wretch,' yelled Pottinger. His men fired, but Gardiner escaped yet again.

This, Gardiner decided, was to be his last scrape. With his lover Kate, Gardiner moved to Queensland, where he became a storekeeper at the Apis diggings, near Rockhampton. Under the name of Christie (which was actually his real name: he had assumed the name Gardiner after an old man who had befriended him in his youth) the ex-bushranger behaved himself. But he was tracked down after 'Mrs Christie' wrote a letter back to her relatives in the Weddin Mountains. On 3 March 1864, Gardiner was arrested and brought back to Sydney, where, on 18 May, he was tried for the attempted murder of Sergeant Middleton.

With a devoted legal team, Gardiner was acquitted. This made headlines throughout the colonies: not only had Gardiner slipped through the police's clutches time after time, now that the police finally had him they couldn't secure a conviction.

The second time, however, the prosecution was better prepared. This time Gardiner was charged with shooting Constable Hosie and the jury found him guilty of wounding with intent to do grievous bodily harm. It was not a hanging offence. Gardiner also pleaded guilty to armed robbery. He was sentenced to thirty-two years in prison. He never saw Kate Brown again. She died soon after travelling to New Zealand with a man described as drunken and quarrelsome.

While in prison, Gardiner's folk hero status was cemented. He had never killed anyone himself and had frequently made the police seem laughable by outwitting them. A consummate rogue, Gardiner inspired letters to the press and debate in Parliament, as a result of which, in 1874, Gardiner and twenty-two other bushrangers were released. As a condition of his pardon, however, Gardiner had to leave Australia.

On his release, Gardiner travelled to San Francisco, where he came to own The Twilight Saloon. One account has it that he died nine years later; other sources say he lived until 1903, when he was finally shot dead during a poker game.

CHAPTER 5

AN HONEST SQUATTER BECOMES NEW SOUTH WALES' MOST WANTED

BEN HALL

If there were any significant women bushrangers, their exploits weren't recorded. Even so, some of the most interesting stories concern the women behind the men.

The Walsh sisters, for instance, were a fascinating trio. Each of them hooked up with a bushranger linked to the 1862 robbery of £14 000 from the Forbes Gold Escort. The eldest sister, Helen, married John McGuire; the youngest, Kate Brown, ran off to Queensland with Frank Gardiner (see Chapter 4). Meanwhile, the middle daughter, Bridget, married an honest and amiable squatter named Benjamin Hall.

By all accounts, it was Bridget's fault her husband turned to bushranging, ultimately becoming the most prolific, daring and infamous outlaw New South Wales had ever seen. His early life certainly gave little indication he would turn to highway robbery. Born near Werris Creek in 1838, Hall was the son of a respected family. Before long he had saved enough pennies to buy himself a small station near Forbes. He was a good law-abiding citizen, so much so that when bushranging arrived in the area in 1861 courtesy of Frank Gardiner, Hall wanted to help the police. To this end, he let groups of policemen stay overnight at his house.

Unfortunately, his hospitality backfired. One of the policemen, a married man named James Taylor, fell in love with Bridget. Hall had his suspicions and he became furious when he found a batch of love letters from his wife's suitor; but, because he loved his wife and their little boy, he forgave her. He had lost her heart, however, and Bridget sensed her chance when Ben and a handful of neighbours left for a few days to track down wild horses. When he returned home, his wife and two-year-old son were gone.

A note had been left. 'You have always been too good a man for me.' It was written by Bridget. 'Poor Ben. Goodbye.' She had run off with her policeman lover.

For three or four days, Hall searched for his wife. 'He abandoned the search in despair and from that day out his life was a reckless one,' wrote Hall's brother-in-law John McGuire many years later. 'I do not wish to invest young Ben with a halo of virtue but until his reckless career began there was probably not a man in the district whom we thought more of.'

That 'reckless career', of course, was bushranging. All of a sudden, Hall had lost his family; not long after, his homestead burnt down. Next, in April 1862, he was surprised to find himself on trial in Orange on a charge of associating with Frank Gardiner. Hall had met the notorious bushranger only once and Hall had been much more of a victim than an associate. The squatter whose life had taken a bizarre turn for the worse was perplexed. He was acquitted, but he was fed up.

Immediately after his acquittal, Hall was staying at McGuire's house when Gardiner came to visit. Gardiner apologised for landing the hapless squatter in trouble. 'Oh, well, it's done now and can't be helped,' Hall replied. 'But the next time they take me, they'll have something to take me for.'

That didn't take long. Hall was arrested after the Eugowra gold robbery of June 1862 (see Chapter 4). Many years later, McGuire said Hall had indeed been involved; but Hall was released not long after his arrest—the police couldn't muster enough evidence to secure a conviction.

Hall became involved with two 22-year-olds, a Canadian, John Gilbert, and a local lad, John O'Meally. Both had spent time bushranging with Frank Gardiner, but now that Gardiner had given up crime and moved to Queensland, Hall took charge. The Ben Hall gang, as the men came to be known, started on a spree of gutsy, daring thievery.

For a year, the trio roamed the highways, fleecing inns, stores, homesteads and travellers and, above all, avoiding the police. First they raided the area between Forbes and Lambing Flat (which later became Young), then they moved to the Carcoar district. On 13 July 1863, Gilbert and O'Meally rode down the main street of Carcoar, stopping at the Commercial Bank, where they drew their pistols and demanded cash from the clerk. Fortuitously for the bank, the manager had been running errands; he returned with the robbery in full swing. Seeing what was happening, he ran to safety, raising the alarm. The bushrangers fled empty-handed, but in and around Carcoar the townsfolk were getting nervous.

Two more gang members were enlisted, Johnny Vane and Mickey Bourke, two exquisite horse thieves. The pair decided to raid the stables of a local magistrate, Thomas Icely, a wealthy pastoralist who owned fine racehorses. Vane and Bourke stole two valuable horses, but were interrupted by a stable hand, German Charley. Shots were exchanged and German Charley was hit in the mouth.

The temperature had risen. Icely offered a £100 reward for the return of his stallion, and police reinforcements poured into the region. In response, Ben Hall relocated his gang to the Junee area. Eventually, however, the inevitable fatality: a storekeeper, John Barnes, travelling between Murrumburrah and Cootamundra, was held up by O'Meally, who wanted his bridle and saddle. Barnes fled; O'Meally chased. O'Meally fired and hit the storekeeper in the back. Barnes died on the spot and the Government responded by offering a reward of £200 for information leading to the arrest of his killer.

In September, the gang committed robberies at Boorowa, Ten Mile, Twelve Mile, Murringo and Blayney. On the twenty-third they stole the uniforms and firearms of three troopers and over the next few days they committed their robberies dressed as mounted police. On the twenty-sixth they arrived at Canowindra, where they bailed up the local residents, but treated them to an all night party in the process. As the *Bathurst Times* said:

> Bushranging by this gang is not followed as a mere means of subsistence. Every new success is a source of pleasure to them and they are stimulated to novelty of actions by their desire to make history. This has become their ambition. They aspire to a name. They combine the desperado and the gallant, and feel that they have built up a superiority which defies the power of the Government. The sympathy which they get from a section of the public builds up their vanity in which they indulge.

The gang's most audacious feat came on 3 October 1863, a Saturday night on which the five members casually rode into Bathurst, population 6000. First they stopped at a gun shop and asked to see the revolving rifles in stock. The shopkeeper had none; could he interest them in Colt revolvers instead? No, said the bushrangers, they already had superior revolvers. They bid their goodbyes before moving on to McMinn's jewellery, a few doors further down. There the gang was in the middle of holding up the shop assistant when they were interrupted by Mrs McMinn, who had been next door. Seeing a gun levelled at the head of her assistant, she screamed, sending the bushrangers fleeing. 'Police!' yelled a handful of onlookers. 'Stop, thief!' Vane shot into the air as the five galloped away.

On horseback, they turned from William Street into Howick Street, then into George Street, where they slowed. Then they rode to the top of the town, to Piper Street, where they held up the publican of the Sportsman's Arms Hotel, stealing his watch and cash box before shouting everyone drinks. Meanwhile, thinking the gang must be headed out of town, every available trooper had set off in pursuit. Only later, when all the fuss had died down, did the gang slip unnoticed out of town.

There were more surprises in store for Bathurst. A few days later, on Tuesday, the gang robbed a series of hotels and stores on the Vale Road, not 2 kilometres from Bathurst. As it happened, the police were right behind—by the last robbery, troopers arrived on the scene only five minutes after the bushrangers had left. The gang's bravado was all the more pronounced given that the head of the New South Wales Police Force (which had only been formed a year earlier) had just arrived in Bathurst with reinforcements to personally oversee the hunt for Hall and to restore the force's morale.

At Canowindra, the bushrangers set up shop at Robinson's Hotel. Again everyone who came through the doors, including fourteen bullock teamsters, was robbed and treated to a party. This time the festivities lasted three days, from midnight on 17 October to noon on the nineteenth, complete with music, dancing, grog and cigars. Johnny Gilbert even brought the local policeman to the celebration.

One of the victims recorded his impressions:

> The whole five are sober youngster—none of them drinks. Gilbert is a very jolly fellow, of slight build and thin—always laughing. O'Meally is a murderous looking scoundrel. Ben Hall is a quiet, goodlooking fellow, lame, one leg having been broken, he is the eldest of the party and the leader—I fancy about 28 years of age. Vane is a big, sleepy-looking man. Mickey Burke [sic] is small …They are constantly talking about their exploits.

Time and again, the authorities were made to look incompetent, until a man named Henry Keightley became the first to stand up to the Ben Hall gang. Keightley, a magistrate and an assistant gold commissioner, upset the bushrangers by speaking out against them publicly. They retaliated by beseiging his homestead near Rockley. During the ensuing shootout, Mickey Bourke was hit in the stomach. Before he could be helped, Bourke put his revolver to his head and pulled the trigger, killing himself.

Livid about the death of their mate, the bushrangers gained the upper hand and forced Keightley to surrender. Vane and O'Meally wanted to kill Keightley, but Hall said they would spare his life if Mrs Keightley rode to Bathurst and brought back a £500 ransom by 2 p.m. the next day. If she was late, they would also kill a visitor, Dr Pechey. She returned just one hour shy of the deadline. Reduced to four members, the gang escaped. The Government responded by increasing the reward for the remaining outlaws to £1000 each, a staggering sum. Ben Hall had suffered his first setback and the inflated reward meant he would have to start being more suspicious of his acquaintances.

What's more, his close friends were dropping like flies. First Vane lost his nerve, surrendering at Carcoar on 19 November 1863. He was sentenced to life in prison. Then, during an attack on a homestead near Eugowra, O'Meally was shot and killed by a couple of squatters desperate to defend their property.

Within one month, five had become two. Unlike Frank Gardiner, however, Hall and Gilbert certainly weren't ready to retire. They headed south, sticking up the Boorowa and Yass mails and committing twenty holdups in a single day, among many, many others. Then, after Gilbert and Hall decided to separate, Hall worked solo before joining up in March 1864 with two new colleagues, Jimmy Dunleavy, aged seventeen, and Tom Gordon. Together, the three robbed travellers and stole horses and had run-ins with the police near Yass before returning to the Forbes area in August.

All the while the net was tightening. In yet another shootout, Hall was wounded and soon he was on his own again. Dunleavy gave himself up and Gordon was captured after trying to go it alone. Then Hall reunited with John Gilbert and the two enlisted a third man, John Dunn, a seventeen-year-old jockey.

On 16 November 1864, the three bushrangers took up positions on the highway south of Jugiong, near Goulburn. They kept themselves busy sticking up passers-by until 3 p.m., when the Gundagai mail appeared. This was exactly what Hall had been expecting. Aboard the coach were a policeman and a driver; accompanying the coach were two troopers on horseback. When the bullets started flying, one policeman fled, two stayed. One of those who stayed was Sergeant Edmund Parry, who was soon shot dead by Gilbert.

The remaining trooper, Sub-Inspector O'Neil, surrendered, leaving Hall, Gilbert and Dunn to plunder the mail and to steal the policemen's horses and firearms. Arrest warrants for murder were issued for all three.

More robberies, more shootouts, more narrow escapes, until the next fatality came at Collector, near Goulburn, on 26 January 1865, during a raid on Kimberley's Inn. The landlord and half a dozen drinkers were being guarded outside by Dunn while Hall and Gilbert

The Ben Hall Gang holding up the Gundagai Mail Coach.

searched inside for valuables. When a horseman approached, Dunn fired a few shots to scare him off. The local lawman, Constable Samuel Nelson, heard the shots. He grabbed his musket and started walking towards the inn. 'Stand! Go back!' yelled Dunn when Nelson came into view. The policeman kept walking; Dunn shot him in the stomach. Dunn fired again, hitting the 38-year-old in the face. Nelson collapsed and died. Two of Nelson's sons, standing nearby, had seen their father shot dead.

Nelson didn't stand a chance, but other victims were not so defenceless. On 6 February 1865, the gang came across a coach driven by the four teenaged Faithfull boys on the Braidwood to Goulburn road. Challenged to stop, George Faithfull whipped his horses into a gallop while two of his brothers returned fire. After a breathtaking chase, the Faithfulls made it back to their Springfield homestead, where they leapt from their coach and sprinted for home, ducking and weaving the bushrangers' bullets. All four were unharmed and the bushrangers retreated.

Ben Hall badly wanted a big haul. On 15 March, with his gang briefly bolstered by the arrival of local outlaw Tommy Clarke (see Chapter 9), Hall struck the Araluen gold escort as it made its weekly winding ascent to Braidwood. On board were four troopers, a gold buyer and a strongbox containing 54 000 grams of gold. On a sharp curve near the top of their climb, Constable Kelly fell from his horse, he had been shot in the chest. Bushrangers! Constable Byrne took up a position behind the wagonette and fired. Constable Kelly propped himself up against the roadside, revolver in hand. The two other troopers ran off into the bush, looping around to surround their attackers. Meanwhile, the gold buyer had set off on foot for help. Sensing they were about to be surrounded, the bushrangers fled empty-handed. Later, Constable Kelly died from his wounds.

It wasn't long, however, before the bushrangers would have even

The scene of Ben Hall's capture and death, near Forbes, New South Wales. Inset: *Ben Hall.*

greater worries: the *Felons Apprehension Act* of 1865. On 10 May, the Government proclaimed that Hall, Gilbert and Dunn would become 'outlaws' and that as such they could be shot on sight without being offered a chance to surrender.

Hall himself had never shot a man, but he was beginning to feel surrounded. He decided to leave the country, but first he visited his wife Bridget and her lover. Hall made Bridget promise that their son Henry would receive Hall's property and any cash he might be able to send.

Benjamin Hall never managed to leave the country. He didn't even make it to 10 May, when he would have become an outlaw. On Thursday, 4 May, Hall was setting up camp by himself at a billabong near Forbes, having returned to the region he knew best. The police had been given a tip-off and Sub-Inspector Davidson lay in hiding with five colleagues and two black trackers. After waiting all night, they ambushed Hall at dawn as he was walking towards his horses. Davidson shot as he pursued the bushranger. He hit. Two other troopers fired and

hit too. Hall was struggling and the troopers kept firing. In total, Hall suffered about thirty gunshot wounds. He died quickly.

When Davidson searched the corpse, he found money and guns. He also found a gold ring on his hand and a portrait of a woman. Davidson didn't specify which woman.

As for Gilbert and Dunn, they took refuge with Dunn's grandfather at Binalong. They shouldn't have, for to claim the reward, Grandpa Dunn gave up his grandson to the police. As a result, five days after Hall was killed, four troopers ambushed the two outlaws. While fleeing, Gilbert was shot through the heart and died. Dunn, however, managed to escape to the Macquarie Marshes in north-west New South Wales. It was seven months before he was found. On Christmas Eve, three troopers recognised him and he was seriously injured in the ensuing gun battle (as was one of the policemen). His recovery was short-lived: on 19 March 1866, John Dunn, aged nineteen, was hanged at Darlinghurst Gaol.

CHAPTER 6

MAD DAN, THE LONESOME KILLER

DANIEL MORGAN

Daniel Morgan had a nickname, Mad Dan. You're probably wondering how he got it.

Well, Morgan was a loner who consistently fell into violent fits of rage, particularly if things went against him. Time after time he behaved irrationally. So it was a succession of events, rather than one specific instance which made people think him crazy. Still, if you had to pin the nickname on one particular day, 19 June 1864 might be it. Not a day that did Dan's reputation for sanity any favours.

It was a Sunday at noon when Morgan showed up at Round Hill station, not far from the New South Wales/Victorian border, with revolvers in hand and additional firepower tucked into his belt. Morgan marched the five occupants of the homestead out to a shed, where a further ten men had already been bailed up by two of Morgan's accomplices. Morgan sent a servant to the house to get grog; she returned with six bottles of gin.

Everyone drank and drank and laughed and had a good time. Eventually Morgan mounted his horse to depart. But before Morgan could go, the station's manager, Sam Watson, made reckless by the drink, asked, 'Are those stirrup irons stolen, Morgan?'

Not very clever. Morgan drew a revolver and shot at Watson, hitting him in the hand. Everyone panicked as the bushranger rode about firing his gun. The son of a neighbouring squatter, John Herriot, was hit in the knee and Morgan rode off to chase another man, who escaped into the kitchen. Then Morgan returned to Herriot and put a revolver to his head. 'For God's sake, Morgan,' cried Watson, crawling from his hiding spot, 'don't kill anyone.'

Suddenly and inexplicably, Morgan's mood changed again. 'Where are the damned wretches?,' he demanded, adding that he would blow out the brains of any man who would not help Herriot. Morgan cut the boot from Herriot's leg and carried him inside to a bed. The station's overseer, John McLean, volunteered to ride to nearby Walla Walla to fetch a doctor. Morgan agreed, telling McLean that he better not ride in the opposite direction, to the police stationed at Ten Mile Creek.

Shortly after McLean left, Morgan became anxious. Could he

trust McLean? The bearded bushranger leapt onto his horse and rode towards Ten Mile Creek. Sure enough, after a few kilometres he came upon McLean. Morgan summarily shot McLean in the side, the ball passing through him and exiting above his navel, knocking him from his horse. Then Morgan helped the station overseer back into his saddle and escorted him back to Round Hill. Morgan left several hours later. McLean died a week after. By now, the newspapers had dubbed their man 'Morgan the Murderer'.

And they'd also dubbed him 'Mad Dan', partly because of his appearance. As Detective Manwaring, the man who eventually caught up with Morgan, wrote:

> He was distinguished by his immense black beard flowing to his breast. His hair hung over his shoulders in gipsy ringlets. His height was nearly six feet. He was stout and muscular but weak in the knees and walked awkwardly. When mounted on horseback he was unsurpassed as a rider …With small clear blue eyes [he had] the appearance of a ferocious bird of prey and a theatrical property man could have made him up into the facsimile of an eagle.

So, what had made him mad? Morgan, who said he was born at Appin in 1830, grew up at Campbell Town, where, even as a youngster, he was considered bad. He worked as a stockman, drifting from place to place until the gold rush of the early 1850s drew him to Victoria. By his twenties he already had a reputation as a horse thief and on 10 June 1854, under the name of John Smith, alias Bill the Native, alias Sydney Bill, Morgan appeared in court on a charge of armed robbery before Justice Barry, the same judge who sentenced Ned Kelly to the gallows sixteen years later (see Chapter 12). Morgan was found guilty and sentenced to twelve years' prison.

In 1860, after serving six years, Morgan was released on a ticket-of-leave. However, Morgan didn't report to police as he was supposed to. Instead he lived a solitary life near the King River, where he became known as Down the River Jack. He stole a few odds and ends and the occasional horse, prompting two local landholders, Evans and Bond, to track him down. They shot and wounded him and Morgan never forgot it.

In the meantime he fled to New South Wales, to the Riverina district near Wagga Wagga and Albury where landholdings were large and isolated. By early 1863 people were starting to hear about a robber named Dan Morgan. Teaming up with a mate, German Bill, Morgan took his criminal skills to the highways.

On 20 August, the pair bailed up a man near Urana. Seeing the bushrangers were on foot, the man dug his spurs into his horse and fled, but Morgan and German Bill leapt onto their mounts and set off in pursuit. After an exhausting chase through thick scrub, the bushrangers had their man. He surrendered. By this stage, Morgan recognised his quarry: Henry Baylis, the Police Magistrate of Wagga Wagga.

'You're none the worse for having met us and if we come before you I hope you'll be easy with us,' Morgan said.

'If you come before me you may depend upon it, I'll do my duty,' Baylis replied.

'You need not mention having met us and we'll say nothing about it.'

'I cannot promise to suppress the matter,' said Baylis. 'I have my duty to do.'

With that, the bushrangers freed the magistrate, who notified the local police as soon as he arrived in Urana. Three days later, Baylis led a party in pursuit of Mad Dan, eventually finding the tracks of two horses and a gunyah (a bush hut) made of bark and saplings. Baylis prepared an ambush. When rain started falling, the party took shelter in the gunyah.

Deep into the night, Baylis heard a noise and went outside to investigate. Then, a gunshot. German Bill had fired at Baylis and missed, but the gun's flash of light had let Baylis know where his attacker was. Two more shots. This time Baylis and German Bill had fired simultaneously. German Bill's bullet passed through Baylis's right thumb and into his right shoulder; Baylis's bullet killed Morgan's mate. Suddenly Morgan appeared beside Baylis. Morgan fired, missing so narrowly that he singed the magistrate's eyebrows and left powder burns on his face. Baylis collapsed and Morgan escaped. The Government responded by offering a reward of £200 for Morgan's capture.

Alone again, Morgan robbed homesteads and travellers. And, like many other bushrangers, during robberies he often asked servants and station hands how they were being treated, telling them to let him know if they were being abused. Morgan wanted to be seen as a champion of the downtrodden, ensuring their co-operation if he ever needed it.

After the irrational antics at Round Hill in June 1864 (described above), Mad Dan headed for a new stamping ground, the Tumbarumba area. On 24 July, Morgan encountered two troopers on the road. Before they even had a chance to recognise him, Morgan had shot Sergeant David Maginnity dead. Trooper Churchley galloped away in fright and he was soon dismissed for cowardice.

The reward for Morgan was raised to £1000 and to £100 for the

Morgan enjoying Mrs McPherson's music.

Sticking up the Goulburn Mail Coach.

conviction of harbourers. But many locals were too afraid to dob in Morgan or his sympathisers. He had already burnt down a woolshed and store at Mittagong station, nearly roasting alive manager Isaac Vincent, whom he suspected of giving information to the police.

Mad Dan was getting madder. When Senior Sergeant Smyth led a party to a swamp where he thought Morgan was hiding, the bushranger had no trouble tracking his trackers. After watching the party for several days, Morgan pounced. Late in the evening of 3 September, while Smyth was reading by candlelight, several shots were fired. Smyth's colleagues rushed out of their tents, but Morgan had already vanished. Smyth died from his wounds a few days later.

For four months, Morgan kept a low profile, relying on his intimate knowledge of the bush to find food and shelter. Suddenly, in early 1865, he was back. And he was busy—on just one day, 15 January, Morgan held up fifteen men at a road contractor's camp, bailed up five Chinese men, shooting one in the arm, stopped two buggies, robbed the mail coach travelling to Albury and the mail coach coming from Albury and finally, at Pulletop, stole £60 from two hawkers.

But, with the help of Aboriginal trackers, the police were closing in. Morgan decided to venture into Victoria, directly challenging the

The death of Morgan.

Victorian Police's boast that he wouldn't last forty-eight hours in their State. During the night of 2 April 1865, Morgan crossed the border near Albury. Guided by moonlight, he stole a racehorse and pressed on. Revenge was on his mind. He wanted to settle the score with Bond and Evans, the two men who had wounded him four years earlier.

Before dawn on 6 April, Morgan arrived at Evans' station on the upper King River, setting haystacks on fire and bailing up everyone who rushed from the homestead. But the man Morgan wanted, Evan Evans, wasn't there.

Morgan helped himself to a hearty breakfast and a fine horse, then hit the road, robbing anyone he encountered. The next morning he arrived at a dairy near Wangaratta, where he asked directions to the Boughyards Station, home of a fine racehorse named Lochinvar. As he was departing, Mad Dan said he was off to bail up the Glenrowan Hotel.

By now, police from Beechworth were hot on his heels, arriving at the dairy only an hour after Morgan left. They correctly guessed that Morgan was not heading for Glenrowan, but to Boughyards. But Morgan never made it there, losing himself instead in dense scrub. Late in the afternoon he bumped into the overseer of Peechelba Station, Robert Telford. Morgan held a gun to Telford's head and told him to lead the way to Peechelba.

They arrived at the station an hour later. 'I am Mr Morgan,' Mad Dan told everyone in the McPherson homestead. 'I suppose you have heard of me?'

With the single, unblinking eye of a pistol trained on them,

everyone in the household was ordered to stand on one side of the room. The panic subsided slightly when Morgan said he only wanted some food and a horse to carry him over the border. Over dinner, however, he made himself comfortable. Morgan had a pleasant chat with Mr McPherson about his exploits, adding that he hadn't slept in five nights. He spoke of going weeks without seeing anyone and obviously enjoyed Mr McPherson's company, staying for hours and entreating her to play the piano. He was clearly very tired.

Meanwhile, two servants slipped out and notified a nearby homestead, who in turn sent a messenger to the police at Wangaratta, 23 kilometres away. Six troopers and volunteers arrived at Peechelba at 2 a.m., and four more police, led by Detective Manwaring, joined them at dawn. Finally, at 8 a.m., Morgan stepped out from the homestead with five other men.

Detective Manwaring had warned his men about firing too soon but as Morgan approached them an over enthusiastic stationhand, John Wendlan (alias John Quinlan), fired a rifle, hitting Morgan in the shoulder. The bullet smashed two vertebrae and left his body at the neck. Mortally wounded, Mad Dan fell to the ground. He was moved to the woolshed, where he died early in the afternoon.

The Coroner, one Dr Dobbyn, had the corpse decapitated, sending the head to a friend for phrenological study, following which the headless bushranger was buried at Wangaratta. As for the reward, Wendlan, the man who had fired prematurely, received £500 and the servant girls who had run for help were awarded a tidy sum. The police received £8 each.

CHAPTER 7

FROM THE WILD WEST TO THE FAR NORTH

MOONDYNE JOE AND JAMES McPHERSON

Western Australia and Queensland were not ravaged by bushranging in the same way as New South Wales and Victoria. In fact, each of these States had but one high-profile bushranger: in the west it was Joseph Johns, alias Moondyne Joe; in the north it was James McPherson, alias the Wild Scotsman. With exploits far removed from those, say, of Ben Hall or Ned Kelly, Joe and James were bushrangers for States with vastly different histories than those of New South Wales and Victoria.

Moondyne Joe became famous, not for bailing up mail coaches or sticking up banks, but for the way he frequently and dramatically gave police the slip.

When the first batch of convicts arrived in Fremantle from England in June 1850, transportation to New South Wales had already ceased. Unlike their predecessors sixty years beforehand, these convicts were treated much more humanely. Most of the new arrivals in Western Australia were given their ticket-of-leave on landing and many had brought wives and children with them.

On 30 April 1853, Joseph Johns was one such new arrival. Although he still had a few years to serve of his ten-year sentence for stealing food, the tall son of a Welsh blacksmith quickly settled into his new environment. And, after his release, Joe soon mastered the ways of the bush, landing work as a fencer and horse breaker. He also tracked down stray horses, returning them to their owners for a reward.

In 1861, though, Joseph Johns was back in trouble. He found a horse without a brand, a 'cleanskin'. As with all cleanskins, he was

supposed to report it to police; instead he marked it with his own brand. On 6 August, he was arrested and imprisoned in the Toodyay town lock-up. When no-one was looking, Johns simply removed the screws supporting the cell door, then freed the horse he had branded from where it was chained in the yard and rode to freedom.

When Johns was recaptured, he was sentenced to three years in jail, which he served quietly. He was released in February 1864. A year and a half later, he was under arrest again, this time on a charge of killing another man's ox. The police claimed Johns was going to sell the carcass. Johns was sentenced to ten years in jail. But the Fremantle Convict Establishment (which is still in use today, but as 'Fremantle Gaol') was barely more secure than the Toodyay lock-up. In August 1866, after five months behind bars, he escaped again. Now known as Moondyne Joe, he was getting something of a reputation, and the police and prison authorities were becoming increasingly irritated.

Police constables and black trackers set out after Joe, catching up to him near present-day Westonia in late September. The escapee was brought back to Fremantle, where he was chained up while a special cell was prepared. The tough-as-nails West Australian Governor, John Hampton, boasted there was no way Joe would be able to escape from this cell. Heavy planks were attached to the cell's stone walls with scores of spikes, while barely any oxygen passed through the mesh grill that covered the small barred window. On a diet of bread and water, Joe was confined to his cell twenty-four hours a day, seven days a week. 'If Moondyne can get out of this,' the Governor gloated on seeing the finished cell, 'I'll forgive him.'

Deprived of oxygen, sunlight and nutritious food, Joe soon became sickly and thin. The prison doctor recommended Joe be given exercise and fresh air, and finally the wardens relented, allowing Joe to break up piles of rock in the prison yard. So, each day, the prisoner went to work. A guard watched Joe, and Joe watched the guard. After several days, Joe noticed that the rocks he shattered were left to pile up until the end of the day, when they were cleared away. Each day Joe would leave in his wake a pile of shattered rocks. As the guard kept a drowsy watch, Joe devised a plan.

Late in the afternoon of 7 March 1867, the warden guarding Joe realised the sound of Joe's sledge hammer had ceased. He was reassured, however, since he could see Joe's hat above the pile of rocks. Maybe the prisoner was taking a break. Eventually the guard went to investigate. His heart sank: there was no sign of Joe, who had hammered a hole in the prison wall and fled. To fool the guard, Joe had balanced his hat on the upturned sledgehammer. 'An express was sent to Perth,' reported the *Perth Gazette*, 'which is said to have greatly disturbed his Excellency and Mrs Hampton's digestion of their dinner.'

For nearly two years, Joe evaded capture. In the end, he was only cornered after a stroke of bad luck. One wet night, Joe made himself comfortable in the wine cellar of Houghton's Vineyard at Upper Swan. Vigneron Charlie Ferguson had spent that same day out and about with some mounted troopers. When the group returned after midnight, Ferguson offered the troopers a glass of wine. Naturally, the troopers accepted. The party entered the cellar. As Ferguson wrote later:

> I lighted a candle I was carrying and commenced to walk along the cellar between the rows of wine barrels … We had only gone a few yards from the door when there was an unearthly yell, and the tall figure of a man, looking extremely weird … sprang out of the darkness. He had allowed his hair to grow in long plaits over his shoulders, and he also grew a very long beard … He had covered his boots with sheep skins to disguise his tracks.

It was 26 February 1869, and Moondyne Joe was back in custody. This time he didn't escape, and when he was released in 1873, he decided to abandon criminal pursuits. In 1879, he married Louisa Hearn, a woman half his age. Joe took up boat-building and, right up to his death in 1900, never had another run-in with the law.

On the other side of the continent, James McPherson, the Wild Scotsman, had a number of things in common with Moondyne Joe. Both were good at escaping; both survived their bushranging days to live relatively long lives; and both, after going straight, ended up marrying women much younger than themselves.

McPherson was anything but your everyday, garden-variety bushranger. Sure, he stole horses and bailed up travellers, but he was also a skilled tradesman educated enough to speak four languages.

One of ten children, James Alpin McPherson was fourteen when his parents arrived at Moreton Bay from Scotland in January 1855. After working as a shepherd, James moved to Brisbane Town with his family, where he embarked on a seven-year apprenticeship to a stonemason. About Christmas 1862, when James was twenty-one, his family moved to a rural property. James stayed behind in the big smoke (which, back then, really wasn't very big or smokey at all). That is when the trouble started, particularly after he had made friends with two petty criminals, Charles Dawson and Charles Morris.

The three worked as shearers throughout rural Queensland until an incident at the remote Cardington Hotel, in the state's north, in March 1864. While Morris waited outside, Dawson and McPherson asked for food, clothing and money. The publican, Mr Willis, thought it was a joke until he found himself staring down the barrel of a revolver. Willis wasn't very impressed. He reached behind the bar for a hammer. In response, McPherson fired, hitting the publican in the cheek. The bushrangers allowed Mrs Willis to tend to her husband while they searched for valuables, which they then tied onto their packhorse. Casually, they made their getaway. The locals were worried, as this part of the country had been free of such crime and the nearest police were three men stationed at Bowen, 200 kilometres to the south. A reward of £100 was offered for the trio's capture.

The locals needn't have been too concerned; McPherson soon left his two mates and headed solo for what was, at the time, the epicentre of bushranging—the western districts of New South Wales. McPherson, it seemed, wanted to join Ben Hall's gang and be in the thick of the action. He wasted no time before having a go. Soon after arriving, the Scottish Queenslander was wanted for stealing a racehorse. Getting away with it, though, was harder in New South Wales, where the police were thicker on the ground. A few days after the theft, McPherson was spotted by a policeman; McPherson galloped away as gunshots flew past his head. The young Scot was unharmed, but shortly afterwards he was not so lucky. This time, on 17 August 1864, McPherson rode right into the path of the bumbling head of western district police, Sir Frederick Pottinger, and an accompanying trooper. Pottinger, the man responsible for leading the hunt against Gardiner, Gilbert and Hall, recognised McPherson and ordered him to surrender. McPherson shot at the two police instead. They shot back, hitting him in the arm. On his trusty stolen racehorse, McPherson was able to escape.

Six months later, a black tracker led police to a camp near Forbes, where they found the Wild Scotsman reading a newspaper. He was arrested and charged for his offences in New South Wales, but the decision was made to return the prisoner to his home State to be tried for the shooting of Willis, the publican. Under armed escort, McPherson was brought to Sydney where, in May, he boarded a paddle steamer for the seven-day trip to Bowen in Queensland. After a preliminary hearing at Bowen, McPherson boarded another steamer for the trip south to Rockhampton, where the proper trial would be held.

Constable Michael Maher accompanied McPherson and the two thoroughly enjoyed each other's company. The policeman, it seems, was impressed with the Scotsman's extensive learning. Who wouldn't trust such a man? At McKay, the steamer pulled in for a two-day stopover. Maher agreed to remove the prisoner's handcuffs, but not his leg irons, to allow him to exercise on the ship's deck. On the first day, there was no problem at all, but on the second day, McPherson disappeared over the railing and into the sea. The next day the leg irons were found in the town with a note attached:

> Presented to the Queensland Government with the 'Wild Scotsman's' best thanks, that gentleman having no further use for them the articles being found to be rather cumbersome to transit in this age of enlightenment and progress—the nineteenth century—many thanks—adieu.

That was on 10 June 1865. It wasn't long before Constable Maher was dismissed from the force.

The Wild Scotsman made good use of his cleverly won freedom. He robbed a mailman at Sandy Creek and a businessmen at Dalby. He bailed up travellers, but mailmen were his preferred target. McPherson robbed one Gayndah mailman three times. Occasionally he pretended to be Johnny Dunn, formerly of the Ben Hall gang, but no-one was fooled. Like several of his bushranging peers, the Scot observed a certain moral code. After stealing the Gayndah mailman's brand spanking new

A black tracker.

saddle, McPherson felt he had gone too far. So he left the saddle at the town of Taroom where he knew the mailman would find it.

Several times the police were painfully close to recapturing their man, but he always managed to elude them—even in December 1865, when he casually trotted into Gayndah to spend a day at the races. The police assembled a posse but McPherson leapt onto his horse and galloped out of town. The posse followed, but the Wild Scotsman successfully slipped away.

On 30 March 1866, McPherson's good fortune left him. Superintendent Nott set a trap, using McPherson's favourite target, a mailman, as bait. McPherson couldn't resist. When he approached the mailman, he saw there was a party following. The bushranger tried to flee, riding down a ridge, but this time the pursuers' horses were fresher. McPherson pulled up his horse and raised his arms in surrender.

McPherson was tied to a fruit tree while word was sent that he had been captured. It was late March 1866. This time the police kept careful guard, diligently escorting their prisoner to Brisbane Gaol,

where he was held until his trial began in August. There was a buzz in the air, would McPherson be sentenced to death? It looked like those clamouring for blood might have their wish granted. The presiding judge for McPherson's trial was Sir James Cockle, the harsh Chief Justice of the Supreme Court.

McPherson enlisted the help of Ratcliffe Pring, a flamboyant barrister who had won a number of apparently hopeless cases. The charge was the felonious wounding of Willis, whose face was still badly scarred two-and-a-half years after he was shot at his Cardington Hotel. Pring sowed the seeds of doubt in the jury's mind—was Willis sure of the identity of the man who shot him? The strategy worked. After deliberating for ten minutes, the jury found the Wild Scotsman not guilty.

The police, however, weren't about to release McPherson. Next he was taken to Maryborough, again on a steamer (Chief Justice Cockle was also on board, and this time the prisoner was kept under tight security), where he was tried for highway robbery. This time he was found guilty and sentenced to fifty years in prison. McPherson's father continued to agitate for his son's release and, in December 1874, the Wild Scotsman, partly thanks to his good behaviour in prison, was freed. It was a condition of release that he could be sent into exile, but this condition was never invoked.

Four years later, when McPherson was still only thirty-seven, he married seventeen-year-old Elizabeth Hoszfeldt. The pair moved to Hughenden, in central Queensland, where they had six children. Ironically, he had given up bushranging, but he still came to a violent end. On 19 July 1895, after attending a friend's funeral, McPherson was thrown to the ground when his horse bolted. Four days later he died, aged fifty-three.

Queen Street, Brisbane, in 1860.

CHAPTER 8

'I AM THE THUNDER ... AND THIS IS MY BOLT.'

FREDERICK WARD

alias CAPTAIN THUNDERBOLT

If you were a bushranger, it wouldn't do to have a name such as John Wimp. Or Bill Bigsoftie. Or Lieutenant Limpnoodle. You had to be tough, so you wanted a name that struck fear into the hearts of the victims you were robbing and the police you were evading.

Hence, there was Mad Dan Morgan and Captain Moonlite, two rugged-sounding rustlers whose names inspired respect. And instead

of the Kelly Family, you had the Kelly Gang. But perhaps the most fearsome name of all belonged to one Frederick Ward, who came to be known as Captain Thunderbolt.

He adopted the name during a robbery in the Hunter region, north of Sydney. Early one morning in December 1863, the tollkeeper at Campbell's Hill on the road between Maitland and

Rutherford was awoken by a relentless banging. Startled, the tollkeeper struggled out of bed and to the gate, where he saw a man with a horse. 'By God,' said the tollkeeper, 'I thought it must have been a thunderbolt.' 'And so it is,' came the reply. 'I am the thunder …' at which point Ward aimed his pistol at the tollkeeper's head, 'and this is my bolt.'

One account has it that Ward later returned both the money and cash box and that he wasn't brandishing a pistol at all but a water tap. But, in the days that followed, Thunderbolt committed more robberies and kept his ill-gotten gains, prompting the *Maitland Mercury* to ask: 'Is this hitherto quiet district to be disturbed as the western district has been for so long a time?' The answer was yes.

The toll-gate robbery was Frederick Ward's first holdup and it took place near where he'd been raised. Ward was born in 1836 at Wilberforce, but at age ten his family moved to Maitland, where young Fred became a proficient horseman and jockey. Perhaps he was a little too fond of fine fillies because whenever he saw a particularly athletic specimen, he simply had to have it. So it wasn't such a surprise when in 1856 he was sentenced to ten years' prison for horse stealing, even though Ward claimed till his death that he was innocent.

On his release, Ward moved to Mudgee, where he eloped with Mary Anne, the Aboriginal wife of an ex-constable. Again, Ward stole two horses. Again, he was arrested. This time it was 1862, and Ward was sentenced to five years on Cockatoo Island in Sydney Harbour, not far from Birchgrove and the present-day Iron Cove Bridge. In September 1863, however, Ward and another prisoner, Frederick Britten, hatched a simple escape plan—they would swim to freedom. And they succeeded, managing to reach the shore without drowning or being eaten by sharks. A reward of £25 was promptly offered for the recapture of the 27-year-old and his co-escapee.

So began Ward's life on the run. Already a fugitive, Ward decided he might as well become a bushranger. Putting aside the morality of the decision, it proved a sensible choice. During a 'career' that lasted seven years, longer than any other bushranger, Ward committed a record number of mail robberies.

From Newcastle to Queensland and as far west as Bourke, people soon learnt of the highwayman with the frightening name. After robbing the tollkeeper, Thunderbolt headed north, sticking up the Warialda mail, stealing horses from various stations and holding up inns at Quirindi, Currabubula and Corrall, among others.

More than a reputation for ferocity, however, Thunderbolt soon became known as a 'gentleman bushranger'. It was said that his pistol was often unloaded during robberies, that he never shot to kill and that he often repaid the money he had stolen. People said he was always polite, never robbed a woman and never took human life.

Anecdotal evidence supports this view, suggesting Thunderbolt behaved like a thoroughly good bloke even while robbing folks of their hard-earned. During one visit to the Spread Eagle Inn at Rutherford Racecourse, Ward said he was hungry and wanted something to eat. The landlady brought him bread and meat. 'How much?' asked Thunderbolt after tucking in. 'Oh, nothing,' she said, 'we never charge for a little thing like that.' Thunderbolt was chuffed: 'Well, I came here to stick you up, but as you're so hospitable, I won't.'

Another anecdote has it that Thunderbolt held up a band of German musicians at a place called Goonoo Goonoo Gap. After ordering the band to play for him, Thunderbolt listened to the band members protest that they were only poor. Thunderbolt still robbed them, but said that if he managed to stick up someone who had won big-time at the Tamworth Races, he would return their money with interest. So, as well as taking £15 from the band, Ward took down their names and addresses. Naturally, the band never expected to see their money again.

They were deeply shocked when they returned to Warwick in Queensland to find a postal order for £20 waiting for them.

Unlike the German band, the authorities were less and less pleased with Thunderbolt's behaviour, and in 1864 the reward for Thunderbolt's capture was raised to £100 and to £50 for any of his associates. As it happened, Thunderbolt worked his way through a stream of associates, generally boys aged between sixteen and twenty. While Thunderbolt remained at large, many of his cohorts were captured or killed, the difference being that Ward was an adept horseman who always ensured his horse was of the highest quality. Some of his accomplices weren't as skilled or lucky. Thunderbolt also had many sympathisers in and around the New England region eager to lend a helping hand.

Which isn't to say there weren't several near misses. On 29 April 1864, the *Tamworth Examiner* reported that Thunderbolt had bailed up the Warialda mail, stolen two horses from a station at Manilla and robbed Munro's Inn at Boggy Creek. Then Thunderbolt and another arrived at Walford's Inn at Millie:

Mr Walford, having been informed of their approach, had hidden away everything of value, so that they got very little, except more grog. The police also had been informed, and three troopers, with a black tracker, soon arrived on the scene. As they approached, the bushranger on guard outside whistled, and the other man came out and mounted, Thunderbolt waving a revolver and pointing to a field behind the house as a challenge. He led his men to the clearing and made a stand. The police followed, and a number of shots were fired on both sides.

The police closed up, and Constable Dalton shot one of the bushrangers, a mere lad, and he fell … [then] the boy raised himself on his elbow and fired. Constable Lynch shot the boy in the neck, probably in time to save Dalton's life. Ward made a dash forward, perhaps with a view to driving the police away from the boy and carrying him off, but the police fire was too brisk, and after a few more rounds the robber turned and rode into the bush.

In 1867, when the Clarke brothers were captured, Thunderbolt became the colony's public enemy number one. The reward for his capture was raised to £200.

Frederick Ward, alias Captain Thunderbolt.

Not only were the police after him, by now Mary Anne was on his tail as well. In fact, Ward's love life was a messy affair from the start. His first love had become ill and was sent to an asylum after Thunderbolt was first sent to prison. In 1866, the police thought they'd tracked down Thunderbolt to a hut between the Manning and Hunter rivers. When they stormed the hut, however, the police found only his other half, Mary Anne, and arrested her.

With his lover in jail, Thunderbolt kept bushranging. On her release, Mary Anne tried to track him down, not knowing that in the meantime he had fallen in love with a woman called Yellow Louisa (or Queen Yellow Long), the part-Aboriginal wife of a settler who lived near Aberdeen. Mary Anne wasn't impressed at all. She gave the police all the information she could about her ex-lover, even volunteering to help track him down.

But it took until 25 May 1870 before Thunderbolt's life of crime finally came to a violent end. Near Uralla, Thunderbolt bailed up an Italian hawker called Giovanni Cappisote and an old man named Williamson. From the former, Thunderbolt stole a gold watch, a gold nugget and some cash. The latter Ward simply accompanied to the local pub, Blanche's Inn, where they drank, danced and sang. Ward told bushranging tales, including the one about the time seven years earlier when he was shot in the leg by police only a few hundred yards from where they were now drinking. This obviously wasn't Thunderbolt's lucky area.

Meanwhile, Cappisote was angry. He drove on before unhitching his horse from its cart and riding to Uralla, where he told Constables Mulhall and Walker what had happened. He was probably hoping to claim the reward, which now stood at £400.

Mulhall reached the inn first and saw Thunderbolt and a young man mount two grey horses. It turned out the young man wasn't a bushranger at all—Thunderbolt had simply stolen one of his horses, so the man was riding along in the hope of having it returned. After shots were exchanged, the young man and Thunderbolt rode off in different directions. While Mulhall tailed the youngster (thinking he was a bushranger), Walker followed Thunderbolt.

At twenty-two, Walker was an accomplished horseman with a lot of local knowledge and this time Thunderbolt's horse was no Phar Lap. After a long and circuitous chase, Thunderbolt turned from the road and rode down the steep hill towards Kentucky Creek. Thunderbolt leapt off his horse and into the river, intending to fool the Constable, remount his horse, then escape. Constable Alex Walker wasn't fooled, however, he shot dead Thunderbolt's horse, then set off in pursuit.

Soon the two were facing each other, standing on opposite sides of

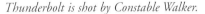

Thunderbolt is shot by Constable Walker.

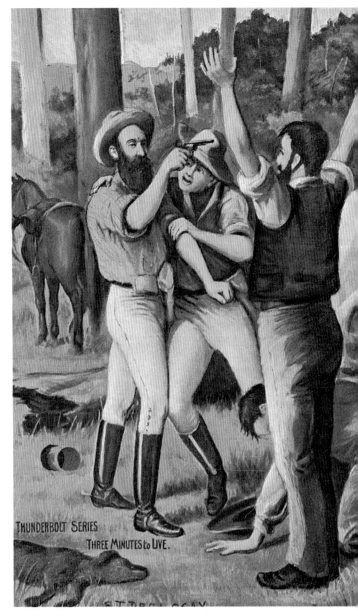

THUNDERBOLT SERIES
THREE MINUTES to LIVE.

Thunderbolt bails up Cappisote and Williamson.

the creek. From his horse, Walker demanded that the bushranger surrender. 'Put your hands up,' Walker yelled. 'Are you a trooper?' asked Thunderbolt defiantly. 'Yes,' was the answer. 'Married?' 'Yes,' said Walker. 'Well,' said Thunderbolt, 'remember your family.'

Walker wasn't about to let Thunderbolt slip away: 'Oh, that's all right,' the constable said. 'Will you surrender?' 'No,' shouted Thunderbolt, 'I'll die first.' Walker replied: 'Then it's you or I for it.'

Constable Walker urged his horse into the river. He raised his revolver and aimed at Thunderbolt. Walker fired. Thunderbolt was hit in the chest. Thunderbolt fell but managed to drag himself up the bank. Walker followed and struck him with the butt of his revolver, knocking Thunderbolt down.

Thinking he had killed the bushranger, Walker dragged Thunderbolt up the steep bank and laid him out on the grass. Then Walker rode off to find help to bring back the body. When Walker's posse returned that evening, however, the bushranger had disappeared, and it was too dark to find any tracks.

The next morning, a trail of blood led the trackers to where Thunderbolt had hidden himself among the bushes. He was taken back to Uralla, but died before nightfall. Thunderbolt was dead. Constable Walker was promoted and received the reward.

CHAPTER 9

THE BRAIDWOOD BUSHRANGERS

THE CLARKE GANG

Throughout the 1800s, police and bushrangers played a dangerous game of cat and mouse. Occasionally, however, it was hard to know who was the cat and who was the mouse.

In February 1866, near Araluen in southern New South Wales, two policemen set up an ambush for a busy group of bushrangers who had become known as the Clarke gang. The officers lay in wait at Morris's store and hotel at Mudmelong. When one of the bushrangers, Tom Connell, casually ambled into the trap, he was promptly arrested.

Meanwhile, however, the rest of the gang had captured another constable from Araluen who had been on his way to assist. With the constable as their prisoner, the gang went to Connell's aid, easily forcing the constables to release the bushranger they had just captured. What's more, the gang took the two policemen prisoner. Having captured three officers, they were on a roll, and when Senior Constable Stapylton from Araluen arrived on the scene, he too was disarmed and arrested by the outlaws.

What could a group of bushrangers do with four captive policemen? The obvious—embarrass them. The outlaws took everything they wanted from the store and forced the luckless lawmen to serve them drinks from the bar. It was midnight before the bushrangers had had their fun and decided it was time to leave. As Constable Woodland, a mounted trooper, recorded, 'This made the police shake their heads dismally, and the civilians too, for the latter began to think it was all up with much of their property.'

So who was this gang that kidnapped and humiliated police officers in southern New South Wales? Well, there were three Clarke boys, Tom, James and John, the children of John Clarke and Mary Connell. Together with some of their mum's family, the Clarke boys embarked on their lawless ways at an early age. But to know the Clarke gang you had to know the area they inhabited, the Jingera mountains around Braidwood. After all, the Clarke gang was originally known as the Jingera Mob.

The Jingera area in the mid-1800s was isolated and rugged, the home of cockatoo farmers and hardened ex-convicts. As Martin Brennan, a police officer who lived in nearby Major's Creek from 1859 to 1862, wrote in his *Police History of Notorious Bushrangers:*

Cockatoo settlers lived all over the Jingera country, on mountains, in gullies, on flats, beside swamps and in extraordinary localities … they occupied the Crown Lands without payment, cultivated no land of consequence and were imbued with a spirit of lawlessness, and never considered there was any difference between right and wrong, where a fat bullock or a good horse was in question.

Yep, it was great country for 'cattle duffing' or 'horse planting' (that is, stealing) and the three young Clarke boys were all good horsemen, excellent bushmen and adept rustlers. What's more, in the 1850s gold was discovered and fields were set up in Araluen, Major's Creek and Nerrigundah. Gold meant easy pickings for the bushrangers—from store owners, travellers and mail coaches.

In mid-1864 a warrant was issued for the arrest of Tom Clarke for horse theft, highway robbery and shooting at three Chinese men. Tom never showed up in court and, after a short stint in Ben Hall's gang, Tom returned to the family business, bushranging.

The law caught up with him in 1865, when the police arrested him at his dad's house and took him to Braidwood Gaol. Behind bars, however, Tommy was surrounded by mates. On 3 October, probably thanks to the help of a corrupt warden, a shoeless Tommy scaled the wall and leapt onto a racehorse that had been conveniently left nearby.

Tommy was out and the crime rate was up. Racehorses went missing and that wasn't all. Folks at Jembaicumbene and Major's Creek were held up; the Michelago Post Office was stuck up; the Araluen Mail was bailed up. The authorities knew who was behind many of the crimes, so a police station was set up at Ballalaba, not 4 kilometres from the Clarke's home. But the police had trouble pinning anything on the Clarke gang. As Constable Woodland wrote:

From this period onwards robberies were committed almost daily, and the people were becoming exasperated. Our party were out every day and every other night, but we could see nothing of them … The bushrangers were getting more daring, the police more impotent, the people more disgusted.

Things deteriorated until February 1866, when the police ambush described at the start of this chapter went laughably wrong.

On 9 April 1866, a beefed-up gang, with Tom Clarke, Pat and Tom Connell, Bill and Joe Berryman, Bill Scott and William Fletcher hit Nerrigundah, the epicentre of the rich Gulph goldfields. Nerrigundah had a population of 600, five hotels and three policemen. When the gang struck, however, one officer was away in Moruya and another, Constable O'Grady, was ill in bed.

Just outside Nerrigundah, at Deep Creek, the gang stopped all passers-by, including a storekeeper from Moruya named John Emmott, who gave up his valuables (he was carrying a gold watch, some silver and nearly a kilogram of gold) only after he was shot in the thigh. He had made the mistake of trying to escape on his horse. Two bushrangers kept the victims under guard; the other five rode into Nerrigundah, robbing passers-by and stores on their arrival.

By now, Constables Smyth and O'Grady (still feeling feverish) had heard what was happening and were heading for Wallis's Hotel. There they found Pat Connell and William Fletcher threatening to shoot the local butcher, Robert Drew, who had irritated the outlaws by throwing a wad of money into the crowded bar, out of their reach. The two constables fired nonetheless. One bullet narrowly missed Connell, the other hit William Fletcher, whom the *Moruya Examiner* described as a young boy of good character. It had been his first attempt at bushranging but the bullet killed him.

Tom Clarke ran after Constable O'Grady and fired at him, hitting him near the heart. Then the gang mounted their horses and made their escape. When O'Grady died a few days later, the reward for the capture of Tom Clarke was raised to £500 and to £300 for Pat Connell. Associates were worth £200 and harbourers £100.

Finally, the police scored a few victories when James Clarke and John Connell were collared for receiving stolen goods; Pat Connell was shot in a police ambush; Bill and Joe Berryman were arrested for armed robbery (their dad was arrested too); and Tom Connell was thrown in gaol. A number of sympathisers and family members were detained for harbouring criminals.

Tom Clarke, however, was still at large, now committing crimes with his youngest brother, John, and Bill Scott, a violent man who had been with the gang during its raid on Nerrigundah. The Colonial

Secretary, Henry Parkes, wasn't impressed. (The Colonial Secretary was the equivalent of today's Premier.) He wanted to wipe out the Braidwood bushrangers. Parkes organised parties of special police, including a party of four volunteers led by John Carroll, a warden at Darlinghurst Gaol.

The game of cat and mouse had just become more complicated. The regular police hated these special police. Wrote Constable Woodland:

> His [Carroll's] presence was the seal and stamp of our incapacity, and we hated him. What ignominy would have been heaped upon us if Carroll's party had been successful!

Well, fortunately for Constable Woodland, Carroll's party wasn't successful. First Carroll and his men disguised themselves as surveyors and pitched camp near the Clarke homestead. When the Clarkes found out what Carroll was up to, they drove him off.

The four volunteers soon returned to arrest a whole swag of sympathisers, but to Carroll's dismay, the sympathisers were all released. Carroll complained that the police were not only ineffective, they were tight with the Clarkes and didn't want Carroll and his volunteers to succeed. He wasn't wrong. The bodies of the four bounty hunters were found in January 1867, about 60 kilometres south of Braidwood. They had been shot dead in an ambush. A £1 note was attached to Carroll's body, a symbol of the blood money he was hoping to earn. The four dead men had money in their pockets which hadn't been touched. According to the *Sydney Morning Herald*, that proved the motive had been revenge, not robbery.

Henry Parkes wasn't happy. Neither were many locals, who criticised local magistrates for being too lenient with the bushrangers. The Government was so unhappy, in fact, that a reward of £5000 was offered for the capture of those responsible for the murder of Carroll and his men. This was a staggering sum, the biggest yet offered for the capture of bushrangers.

About 150 active officers were now scattered throughout the Braidwood area. Nonetheless, the Clarkes continued on their crime spree throughout January, February and March, robbing travellers, stores and mail coaches. On 9 April, the corpse of gang member Bill Scott was found; an inquest found he had 'met his death by foul play'. In other words, the Clarkes probably shot him. Tom and John Clarke were on their own. What's more, some of their family and friends had started to inform on them, especially after the reward was raised to £1000 for the capture of Tom and £500 for John.

Tommy Clarke escapes from prison, 1865.

Constables O'Grady and Smith repulse the Clarke gang at Nerrigundah in April 1866.

On 26 April 1867, a black tracker named Sir Watkin Wynne led Senior Constable William Wright and four policemen to a hut near the house of Thomas Berry. The six men arrived at 8 p.m. and hid themselves behind a haystack. And they waited. Despite the heavy rain, they waited.

Finally, after dawn, Tom and John Clarke emerged, but they didn't come the way Wright had expected. 'Look out,' one of the bushrangers yelled, 'There's someone behind the stack.' They turned and ran. Wright ordered them to surrender. They didn't, and the police opened fire. The bushrangers drew their revolvers and fired back as they fled. John was struck in the shoulder, but continued to run. One officer, Constable Walsh, was hit in the hip; Sir Watkin was hit in the arm, which was later amputated.

The bushrangers fell back into the hut. They took a look at John's wound. It was serious. The bullet had struck him in the arm and brushed his shoulder blade before flying out of his back. In their hardwood hut, the outlaws had plenty of protection and plenty of guns (including revolving rifles, double-barrelled guns, pistols and revolvers). They were set for a shootout.

But Senior Constable Wright was happy to wait. He sent one of his men back to Ballalaba for reinforcements, which arrived soon after noon. One account has it that the Clarkes surrendered when they realised how badly they were outnumbered; another says the policemen stormed the hut and forced the Clarke brothers to give up. Either way, later that day both men were handcuffed and arrested. The Clarke gang was no more.

The bushrangers were brought to Sydney, where crowds were surprised to see 'two sheepish-looking, overgrown youths' instead of psychotic killers. In late May, the brothers appeared before Sir Alfred Stephen, charged with wounding Constable Walsh with intent to kill. They were found guilty and hanged in Darlinghurst Gaol on 25 June 1867.

In his judgment, Sir Stephen said:

> Others who may think of commencing a course of crime like yours may rely on it that better days are coming, and that there will be no longer that expression of sympathy with crime which sometime since disgraced this country, and sunk it so low in the estimation of the world.

Meanwhile, the middle brother, James Clarke, had been sentenced to seven years' prison in 1865. As it turned out, he was the lucky one, avoiding the unpleasant fate of Tom and John.

As usual, the police had played the part of the cat and, as usual, the cat had won in the end. Since no-one ever proved who had murdered Carroll and his three men, the Government never even had to pay out the £5000 reward.

CHAPTER 10

A CHARISMATIC CON MAN TURNS BUSHRANGER

ANDREW GEORGE SCOTT

alias CAPTAIN MOONLITE

Most bushrangers won notoriety for their criminal exploits in Australia. Andrew George Scott, however, had only a very brief bushranging career. Most of this confidence trickster's exciting adventures happened before he even arrived in Australia.

Born in Ireland in 1842, Scott moved to London as a teenager to study engineering, but soon became restless. By his own account, he travelled to Italy in 1860, where he fought alongside Garibaldi's red shirts before sailing for New Zealand. There he claims to have enlisted in the Volunteer Defence Corps, fighting against Maoris in the Waikato War. Then he apparently travelled to the United States to fight in the Civil War. Sounds exciting, but Scott was a silken-tongued con artist, so his account has to be taken with a grain of salt. When he was admitted to prison in Melbourne in 1872, however, an examining officer recorded several gun shot wounds, on Scott's left breast, right foot, and both shins. He had clearly been involved in at least one shootout.

Whatever the truth about his past, the itinerant Scott arrived in Sydney in January 1867. Before long he had relocated to Melbourne and thence to Egerton, a gold town of 4000 near Ballarat. Brandishing fake letters of introduction, Scott was appointed a lay minister, gradually befriending James Simpson, a schoolmaster and Ludwig Brunn, an agent for the London Chartered Bank. Scott noted carefully that Brunn handled a lot of gold, storing it at the bank's premises on the main street.

At 8 p.m. on 8 May 1869, Brunn was in the banking chambers where he kept the gold. In walked a man wearing a mask. 'Take me inside,' said the man, motioning to where the valuables were kept. Brunn recognised the voice of the minister. 'Why, Mr Scott,' said Brunn, 'surely you're taking the joke too far.' 'Who's Scott? I'm Captain Moonlite,' roared the masked man. Brunn saw the man was holding a revolver, so he opened the safe as he was told. The masked thief was pleased to grab £697 in cash and £518 worth of gold, including one large, identifiable ingot.

Then the gunman marched Brunn to the schoolhouse, forcing the distressed banker to write a note. 'I hereby certify,' said the note, 'that L.W. Brunn has done everything in his power to withstand our intrusion and the taking away of the money which was done with firearms.' The note was signed, 'Captain Moonlite.' After tying up and gagging Brunn, the man who called himself Moonlite was gone.

The next day Preacher Scott received a visit from the police. Apologetically, the police said Brunn had accused Scott of the theft. Scott laughed and coolly examined the note written during the robbery. He nonchalantly said the robber's signature resembled the handwriting of James Simpson. Scott's ruse worked, Brunn was charged with the robbery; Simpson as an accomplice. Fortunately for the schoolmaster and the banker, due to insufficient evidence both were acquitted.

By the time of the trial, Scott was already back in Sydney, this time with a new identity. Now he was telling anyone who would listen that he was a squatter with large properties out west. He spent lavishly, particularly on an ocean-going yacht. Scott partly paid for the boat with a cheque for £150. When the vendor discovered the cheque was worthless, he contacted the police. After some quick inquiries, they

discovered Scott had set sale for Fiji not long before. The police set off in pursuit. Scott had just sailed out of Sydney Harbour when a police steamer caught up with him. Scott was arrested and charged with fraud.

Scott had piercing, passionate eyes and was extremely charismatic and eloquent; he could sell sand to a lifesaver. During his trial, he was confident enough to conduct his own defence. Nonetheless, the evidence was overwhelming, and Scott was sentenced to eighteen months in prison.

What's more, after discovering that Scott had sold the ingot that had been stolen in Egerton to a Sydney dealer, Victorian police came to suspect Scott had done the Egerton bank robbery. As soon as Scott was released from Parramatta Gaol in March 1872, Victorian Police arrested him and extradited him to Ballarat to stand trial. Shortly after he arrived at Ballarat's new gaol, however, the engineering knowledge Scott had gained in London proved useful. First, he cut a hole in the wooden wall separating his cell from the next—now he and a prisoner named Dermoodie were in one cell together.

The two broke the lock and escaped into the corridor and waited for a passing guard. When one came, the prisoners overpowered him, bound and gagged him and stole his keys. Quietly, Scott released four more prisoners and told them to bring their blankets. He had crafted a plan. When the six men reached the prison wall, they tore the blankets into strips, which they tied together to form a rope. To get over the wall, the men climbed onto each other's shoulders, then hoisted up the remaining men with their makeshift rope.

The escape went smoothly, but soon all six escapees were recaptured, Scott after a few weeks at large. So, finally, in July 1872, more than three years after it happened, Scott was put on trial for the Egerton robbery. Halfway through the eight-day hearing, Scott dismissed his lawyer, conducting the rest of the defence himself. Once again, Scott was articulate and impassioned; once again, he was found guilty. This time he was sentenced to ten years' prison for the robbery, plus one extra year for his Ballarat escape.

In Melbourne's Pentridge Prison, Scott behaved himself. As a result, he was released early, after seven years, in March 1879. Then, in yet another career change, he took to public speaking, lecturing about life inside and prison reform.

From June 1872 to April 1878, Australia had been free of bushrangers. During this period, the police congratulated themselves on their successes and travellers went about their business in safety. In 1878, however, bushranging had its final outbreak. First, Ned Kelly arrived on the scene (see Chapter 11); next Scott abandoned public speaking for the life of the highwayman.

With his powerful personality, he recruited five youngsters: James Nesbitt (alias Lyons), twenty-four, a friend from prison who had become Scott's right hand man; Thomas Rogan, twenty-two; Graham Bennett, twenty; Augustus Wreneckie, nineteen; and Thomas Williams, nineteen. They headed north. On Saturday 15 November 1865, the party of six arrived at Wantabadgery station, between Wagga Wagga and Gundagai in southern New South Wales, a beautiful riverfront property with hundreds of sheep and cattle, thirty-nine horses and a lush orchard.

The Wagga police arrive at the Wantabadgery station.

Fully armed, Moonlite ordered the women to cook a meal and the men to give up their firearms. Whenever anyone arrived at the door, they were immediately robbed and put under guard. When one particular prisoner irritated him, Moonlite was overcome with rage, he pushed the man into the dining room, forced him onto his knees and asked whether he wanted to die by knife or by pistol. It was only after a lot of begging and pleading that Moonlite relented.

On Sunday morning, several more arrivals took the number of captives to thirty-five. Spying the thoroughbred of a new prisoner, Moonlite grabbed the reins and tried to leap onto the filly's back. But the horse had other ideas, rearing and bucking violently. Moonlite went into another rage, shooting the horse dead. In his own bizarre way, Moonlite was having fun and he decided to put one of the prisoners on trial for 'unlawfully carrying firearms'. Moonlite played the role of judge; the jury was a mix of bushrangers and prisoners. Eventually the accused was found not guilty, which was lucky. 'If the jury had found you guilty,' Moonlite said, 'I'd have given you five minutes to live.' Next the inventive outlaw went for a ride in a buggy, bringing back more prisoners to the homestead at Wantabadgery.

The bushrangers' vigilance was becoming lax, however. On Sunday afternoon, one of the prisoners escaped and alerted the police at Wagga Wagga, 25 kilometres away. When four police arrived at the homestead just before dawn on Monday, one of the station's dogs started barking. Brandishing a double-barrelled gun, Moonlite stepped outside. 'Stand in the Queen's name!' barked one of the troopers. Instead, Moonlite fired, then disappeared back inside. According to the version of events given by Senior Constable Rowe, the bushrangers then rushed from the house, firing as they went. Narrowly avoiding being surrounded, the troopers retreated so far

that the bushrangers were able to steal the police horses. In serious trouble, the policemen fled.

At 9.30 a.m. the bushrangers, riding their stolen mounts, left Wantabadgery. Heading for Gundagai, they bailed up whomever they encountered before resting at McGlede's farm to get milk.

At 11 a.m. five police from Gundagai, two armed volunteers and the four Wagga troopers (who in the meantime had found four new horses for themselves) arrived at Wantabadgery. Finding out the direction Moonlite had taken, they galloped off in pursuit. 'I am determined on capturing the bushrangers, or die in the attempt,' Senior Sergeant Carroll told his men. 'We are well armed. The eyes of the country are upon us and the reputation of the police service lies in our hands.'

The police, followed by about three hundred stickybeaks who wanted to witness the impending confrontation, caught up with the outlaws at McGlede's farm. Moonlite was ordered to surrender. 'Surrender be damned!' he yelled, setting off a bloody gunfight. The bushrangers hid behind fences while the police tried to surround them. Most of Moonlite's men retreated inside, except Wreneckie, who fired at Trooper Barry, but missed. As Wreneckie turned to run, Barry shot the nineteen-year-old bushranger in the back.

Then someone, probably Moonlite himself, shot Trooper Bowen in the neck. Bowen died at Gundagai some days later. Two police rushed into the house. Nesbitt was hit in the temple, Bennett in the arm. The police found Williams trying to hide in the chimney (Williams hadn't been a very competent bushranger. He couldn't ride, and he didn't know how to load a gun). Rogan, however, had disappeared. The bushrangers surrendered, and when Moonlite saw Nesbitt's terrible wound, he fell to the floor at his side. 'Will he really die? He is my only dear friend.' Nesbitt and Wreneckie died soon afterwards, and Moonlite, Bennett and Williams were arrested. Rogan was found the following day hiding under Miss McGlede's bed.

The four men were tried in Sydney for the murder of Constable Bowen. Moonlite addressed the jury for hours, invoking every ounce of persuasiveness he could muster. Hoping to postpone the trial, he pleaded:

Coming to the railway line the stations were crowded with people hooting and crying for our blood. The jury cannot be in a fit condition of mind to undertake the calm consideration of this case, which involves our lives.

Despite the eloquent bushranger's best arguments, the trial went ahead and Moonlite was sentenced to death. From his cell at Darlinghurst Gaol, he continued to protest his innocence and victimisation until minutes before he was hanged at 9 a.m. on 20 January 1880. Rogan was hanged with him; Bennett and Williams were thrown into prison.

Chapter 11

BUSHRANGING'S FIERY CLIMAX

NED KELLY

Part I: NED GETS MAD

Like many good stories, the history of bushranging in Australia saves the best for last.

Ned Kelly was the defiant outlaw weathering a barrage of bullets in the homemade armour with slits for eyes. He was the man who

came to symbolise (whether rightly or wrongly) the ideal of the Aussie battler: distrustful of authority; loyal to his mates; irrepressibly courageous. His iconic status was enshrined by the art of Sidney Nolan, countless books and a tide of films. He was the man who, over the years, became the single most identifiable figure in Australian history. After all, which other Australian can boast that, in the movie made about their life, their role was played by Mick Jagger?

Ned Kelly, the last of the bushrangers. By the time Ned had turned to robbing banks, pursuing a career as an outlaw had become almost impossible. Thanks to the young but improving police force (in both New South Wales and Victoria), improved communications (courtesy of the telegraph and trains) and better firearms, bushrangers were easier to track down and capture. Indeed, between 1872 and 1878 Australia was bushranger-free. For six years it appeared as if the last highwayman had come and gone. Not so. Still to come were Captain Moonlite (see Chapter 10) and, most dramatically of all, the Kelly gang.

John Kelly was an ex-convict who, in 1850, married an Irish immigrant named Ellen Quinn. In June 1855 they had their first son, Edward Kelly. Edward, or Ned, wasn't even a teenager when, in 1865, his father was convicted of the illegal possession of a hide and sent to Kilmore gaol. When his father died late in 1866, Ned was only twelve. With his dad gone, Ned had no choice but to leave school and take responsibility for feeding his family, which now comprised his mum Ellen and six brothers and sisters: Jim (born 1856); Dan (1861); Kate Kelly; Grace Kelly; and the two sisters who would marry to become Mrs Skillian and Mrs Gunn.

Still grieving over John Kelly's death, the Kelly family moved to Eleven Mile Creek, near Benalla in Victoria. 'They all appeared to be existing in poverty and squalor,' wrote Superintendent Nicholson, the man who went on to lead the hunt for Ned and Dan after they'd become outlaws. '[Mrs Kelly] lived on a piece of cleared and partly cultivated land on the roadside in an old wooden hut with a large bark roof. The dwelling was divided into five compartments by partitions of blanketing, rugs, etc.'

Struggling to provide for his family, Ned soon found himself facing criminal charges. First, in 1869, the fourteen-year-old was charged with violently robbing a merchant, Ah Fook. The case was dismissed. Then, in May 1870, Ned appeared in court after he was recognised as an accomplice of bushranger Henry Power. Ned faced two charges of robbery under arms, but was again acquitted for a lack of evidence.

In Victoria in the 1860s, the land was divided between the squatters (the rich, established landholders) and the selectors (the poorer newcomers). Rivalry between the two groups was intense, and the selectors often felt the police were acting against them on behalf of the squatters, who were rich enough to offer substantial rewards if, say, a couple of their cattle went missing. As selectors, the Kellys were among those who felt persecuted.

Starting in September 1870, Ned did his first stint in prison after sending a pair of calf's testicles and an obscene note to a hawker's wife. Ned and the hawker had been arguing over the hawker's cart; Ned, now fifteen, was sent to Beechworth Gaol for six months. Soon after he was released he was sentenced to another three years after he was caught with a stolen horse.

After serving his time, Ned kept his nose clean for three years, working his way up to become overseer of a timber mill near Mansfield. For a period, then, it looked as if Ned and the law might be able to leave each other alone. The outlook was pleasant. Pleasant, that is, until Constable Fitzpatrick came to visit, a gun was fired and Ned and his young brother Dan found themselves suddenly destined to a life of bushranging.

The incident came about when, in 1877, warrants were issued for Dan's arrest on six charges of horse stealing. Dan had just served three months for housebreaking, but this time the police couldn't find him. Finally, on 15 April 1878, Constable Alexander Fitzpatrick, hearing Dan was hiding out at home, went to visit the Kelly residence at Eleven Mile Creek. Fitzpatrick was contradicting an instruction to all police not to visit the Kelly residence alone. The constable had also been flirting with Kate Kelly, which Ned and Dan Kelly weren't happy about. Worst of all, Fitzpatrick had been drinking.

When Fitzpatrick rode up, Dan was standing at the door. 'You're my prisoner,' said Fitzpatrick. Dan nonchalantly agreed, but said he was hungry and wanted to eat before he would go to Benalla, which was 18 kilometres away. The constable said he would wait and started following Dan inside.

As soon as Dan's mother saw the constable, she reddened with rage. 'You won't take Dan out o' this tonight,' the fiery Mrs Kelly exclaimed. 'Shut up mother,' said Dan, 'it's all right.' As she was putting bread and meat on the table, she turned to the policeman again, 'Have you got a warrant?' she demanded. 'I've got a telegram,' replied Fitzpatrick, 'and that's as good.' Dan was in a less aggressive mood, inviting the constable inside to share his meal, but Mrs Kelly continued to fume. 'If my son Ned was here,' she said as Fitzpatrick was sitting down, 'he'd throw you out of the window.' 'And here he is,' said Dan. Fitzpatrick turned to look.

As Fitzpatrick turned, Dan pounced on him. The feisty Mrs Kelly grabbed a shovel and hit the constable over the head, seriously denting his helmet. Hearing the noise, in rushed Ned Kelly, William Skillian (husband of one of the Kelly daughters) and William Williams (a neighbour). Ned had a gun. He fired, hitting Fitzpatrick in the wrist. The constable reached for his revolver, but Dan had already snatched it from its holster. 'I'm sorry I fired,' said Ned. He said Fitzpatrick wouldn't be allowed to leave until the bullet had been cut out and the constable had promised not to tell who had shot him. 'Tell him if he does tell he won't live long after,' yelled Mrs Kelly.

The constable had little choice but to let Ned cut out the bullet with a pocket knife. Then the injured trooper was allowed to leave. The next day, at Benalla, his wounds were treated by a doctor, who noted that the constable smelled of brandy. Meanwhile, a party of troopers arrived at the Kelly homestead, where they arrested Williams, Skillian and Mrs Kelly. The two men were sent to prison for six years for assaulting Fitzpatrick; Mrs Kelly was sentenced to three years.

Ned and Dan, however, had fled to the Wombat Ranges near Mansfield, where they built themselves a bullet-proof hut using chunky logs. They fossicked for gold and grew barley to distill whiskey, working to raise money for another trial for their mother. The lads were deeply devoted to their mum and both offered to surrender in exchange for Mrs Kelly's release. The police, though, weren't about to let a Kelly, and that included Mrs Kelly, go free. Instead, twenty-five troopers set off to track down the fugitives.

Weeks dragged into months and there was still no sign of the brothers. Indeed, six months had passed since the incident at Eleven Mile Creek and the police were looking increasingly incompetent when, on 25 October 1878, four police led by Sergeant Kennedy set out for the Wombat Ranges. The four, all Irish, were considered the best men in the Victorian Police Force. They camped that night at Stringybark Creek, not knowing how near they were to Dan and Ned's hideout. Unfortunately for the troopers, the Kellys had been warned that Sergeant Kennedy was on his way.

When he woke the next morning, Kennedy set out with Constable Scanlan to look around. Constables Lonigan and McIntrye stayed behind. Later that day, Lonigan was brewing a pot of billy tea when he was startled by a loud voice: 'Bail up!' It was Ned Kelly. 'Hold up your arms!' McIntyre obeyed; Lonigan leapt for cover and drew his gun. Briefly raising his head to aim, Lonigan was shot by Kelly. Before dying, the policeman had time only to yell, 'Oh Christ, I'm shot.'

Ned and Dan weren't operating alone. Two mates had joined them: Steve Hart, an eighteen-year-old expert horseman who had served eighteen months for horse stealing and Joe Byrne, a tall 21-year-old who had served six months (together with his friend Aaron Sherritt) for possession of a stolen cow hide. The gang held a gun to McIntyre's head, telling him to convince the other two officers to surrender. If they surrendered, the three police would be allowed to walk back to Mansfield, minus their weapons and horses, of course.

McIntyre did as he was told, but when Scanlan and Kennedy returned, Scanlan thought McIntyre was joking. Scanlan put his hand to his belt and laughed. Ned leapt from behind a log, ordering the constables to 'Bail up!' Instead, Scanlan leapt from his horse and tried to find cover in the thick scrub. Ned fired at the constable. He missed. Scanlan fired back, but missed too. Ned's next shot killed the constable. Kennedy, meanwhile, spurred his horse into a gallop, but was knocked from the saddle by a rifle shot. He tried to take shelter behind his horse, but it bolted towards McIntyre. Seizing the opportunity to escape, the unarmed McIntyre leapt onto Kennedy's mount, but before he made it far the horse was brought down with a fatal shot to the heart.

Refusing to surrender, Kennedy kept firing as he dodged from tree to tree. Ned's aim, however, was true. First he hit the constable in the armpit, then near his heart. The constable, whom Ned later described as 'the bravest man I have ever met', was dying. Ned walked up to him and shot him through the heart to put him out of his misery. Meanwhile, McIntyre was nowhere to be found. The four outlaws searched and searched, but to no avail. Eventually, they gave up.

Scratched and exhausted, McIntyre turned up at Mansfield the following day, telling how the other three constables had been shot dead. The bloody incident was reported far and wide to a horrified public. Were the bad old days of bushranging back? McIntyre also told how he'd escaped: after he was thrown from his horse, he'd scrambled down a wombat hole. He'd lain there quietly for hours before making his getaway.

The reward for the capture of Ned and Dan was raised to £500 each; the identities of Steve Hart and Joe Byrne, however, were still unknown.

The police soon lost all trace of their quarry, who were superior horsemen and more familiar with the tricky terrain. As the weeks became months, the police tended to make modest expeditions into the bush from the railway line or main highways, whereas the Kellys carefully avoided the main thoroughfares.

Ned and his gang disappeared until 9 December 1878, when a dishevelled bushman appeared at Younghusband's station at Faithfull Creek asking after the manager. The bushman was told the manager was out. 'I'm Ned Kelly,' the bushman told Mrs Fitzgerald, the wife of an old station hand. 'But you needn't be frightened, we only want food for ourselves and our horses.' Of course, Mrs Fitzgerald was a little frightened. 'This is Mr Kelly,' she told her husband. 'He wants some refreshments.' Mr Fitzgerald saw Ned had a gun in his hand. 'Well, if the gentleman wants refreshments, he'll have to have them.' With that, Ned whistled and his three friends appeared.

In fact, the gang wanted more than refreshments; their arrival at the station was stage one of a carefully-constructed plan. First the bushrangers rounded up everyone working on the station, locking them in a storeroom. Then, when a storekeeper named Gloster arrived on a cart loaded with goods for sale, he was forced to surrender too. Next the station's manager, Macauley, returned home. Macauley wondered why the gang didn't just take what they wanted and leave. Ned said he had a purpose. What he didn't say was that the gang had chosen Younghusband's station as a base for a raid on the town of Euroa, 6 kilometres away. The previous day Steve Hart had visited the town of three hundred, noting the exact location of the bank and police station.

Back at the Younghusband's, Joe Byrne guarded the swelling number of prisoners (which now included kangaroo hunters and railway workers), while the three other outlaws cut the telegraph wires which might be used to contact police. Then, on Tuesday, 10 December, the three headed into town, Ned driving the cart stolen from the kangaroo hunters, Dan following in the hawker's cart and Steve Hart riding alongside on horseback.

It was about 4.30 p.m. when Ned knocked on the door of the National Bank at Euroa, which had just closed its doors for the day. After a bit of pleading, Ned convinced the manager, Mr Scott, to let him in to cash a cheque. As soon as he was inside, Ned announced who he was and, with the help of Steve Hart, bailed up Scott and two tellers. Then Ned went into the adjoining living quarters and took captive Scott's wife, mother-in-law, seven children and two servants. Altogether, the bushrangers pocketed £2000 worth of gold and cash before telling all their prisoners to board the carts outside. As the procession calmly passed through town, the outlaws forced their prisoners to behave as if they were enjoying a happy family outing. No-one in Euroa who saw the convoy had the slightest inkling a robbery was taking place; apparently Mrs Scott even had trouble believing this man, with his perfect manners, was the dreaded Ned Kelly of Stringybark Creek fame.

The carts were led back to Younghusband's station, where the outlaws were in a jovial mood. A couple of them performed a display of trick riding, while Ned harped on about the way his family had been methodically victimised by police. Ned tried to justify his shooting of Constable Fitzpatrick and his actions at Stringybark Creek. Then Ned gave Mrs Fitzgerald a bulky envelope addressed to a Victorian politician, Donald Cameron, who Ned hoped would be sympathetic. In the envelope was Ned's side of the story, but Cameron turned out not to be very sympathetic at all. Cameron edited the document, removing the charges Ned made about the police. In the end, the tract did little to arouse support for the Kellys.

At 8 p.m., the bushrangers said their goodbyes to their captives at Younghusband's. 'If anyone leaves within three hours, I'll shoot him dead,' said Ned. 'I can track you anywhere in this country and I'm a man of my word.' And with that, the four were off, £2000 richer. They hadn't fired a single shot.

Confidence in the police was plummeting. At police headquarters in Benalla, an exhausted Superintendent Nicholson was replaced by Superintendent Hare, who began to cultivate a network of informers. Unfortunately, many of these informers supplied false information, so the police were rushing about furiously but getting nowhere fast.

The gang of four disappeared from view until a raid in February 1879 put them back in the headlines. This time Ned's target was a small New South Wales town called Jerilderie, the quiet, isolated home of four hundred on the Yanco Creek. It was a town of one bank and two police officers. At midnight on 8 February, the bushrangers surprised the two sleeping police officers, locking them in their own cells and taking their uniforms. All the following day the bush-rangers, wearing the stolen uniforms, wandered freely about town. The locals mistook them for visiting troopers.

After a restful night's sleep in the police barracks, Ned had the unarmed Constable Richards take him to the Royal Hotel. There Ned quietly herded the crowd into one large room where Dan Kelly kept watch. Again, the gang had done its homework. The yard of the hotel backed onto the rear of the Bank of New South Wales and there was no fence between the two properties. Joe Byrne casually strolled into the bank via its back entrance, pointed a pistol at a teller's head and led all three bank officials back to the hotel.

At this point Ned ordered drinks for everyone, exclaiming once again that all of this inconvenience was the fault of Constable Fitzpatrick. Then he returned to the bank and pocketed £2141 in cash. While Ned was in the bank, three customers came in. Realising what was happening, they turned and fled. Ned only managed to capture one of them, and he was furious to learn that one of the men who'd escaped was Gill, a newspaper editor. Ned had compiled a fifty-seven-page defence of himself and his family which he had wanted Gill to publish. One of the bank's tellers promised to hand it on to Gill. Ned trusted him, but the teller didn't keep his word. The document became known as the 'Jerilderie Letter', and in it Ned revealed his one-eyed hatred of the police, describing them as 'a parcel of big ugly fatnecked wombat headed big bellied magpie legged narrow hipped splay-footed sons of Irish Bailiffs or English landlords which is better known as officers of Justice or Victorian Police.'

Back at the hotel, Ned was told that Hart had stolen a reverend's watch. 'What right has a thing like you to rob a clergyman?' Ned asked. Ned made Hart return it.

Meanwhile, if anyone in town who hadn't been taken prisoner had known what was going on, they couldn't have done much about it.

The National Bank of Australia, Euroa, Victoria, robbed by the Kelly Gang in December 1878.

As at Younghusband's station, the gang had cut the town's telegraph wires. Just to be sure, they'd also chopped down seven telegraph posts.

For four days, from Saturday midnight until 4 p.m. Wednesday, the Kelly gang held the town of Jerilderie. As in Euroa, not a shot was fired and no-one, apart from the bank, was robbed. More than once Ned threatened to kill someone for betraying the gang, but he never acted on his threats. The raid was carefully planned and carefully executed and, when it came time to leave, Ned freed all the prisoners, whereupon he and his three partners-in-crime rode off in different directions, confusing anyone who might try to follow.

At Euroa, the gang had made the Victorian Police look stupid; at Jerilderie, the New South Wales Force was made to look equally inept. The New South Wales Government declared the four gang members outlaws, offering a £3000 reward for their capture, dead or alive. The Victorian Government matched this reward. The banks of New South Wales and Victoria offered another £2000 for good measure. At a total of £2000–£8000 per man, it was the highest reward ever offered for the capture of bushrangers. It was a staggering sum, but for a while it looked as if it might never be claimed. Soon the four outlaws were safely tucked away in their hideaway in Victoria's Strathbogie Ranges.

CHAPTER 12

BUSHRANGING'S FIERY CLIMAX

NED KELLY

Part 2: NED BECOMES AN ICON

Ned Kelly, although a murderer, fulfilled something of a national dream,' writes Keith Dunstan in his book, *Saint Ned.* 'For two years he and his three young comrades outwitted an entire police force, made it look ridiculous, then died with courage. Of such stuff legends are made.'

The legend came later, however. While Ned was still alive, many Australians feared and hated the outlaw. And, for more than a year after the Jerilderie heist of February 1879, it looked as if Ned might live for a long time yet. Soon after their two daring, successful raids, first on Euroa, then on Jerilderie, Ned Kelly, Dan Kelly, Steve Hart and Joe Byrne were safely hidden away in the dense and difficult Strathbogie Ranges. Perhaps the four fugitives could avoid a violent end. Perhaps there was no need for dying with courage after all.

The police were growing more and more frustrated, and Superintendent Hare wasn't helping. Under the Outlawry Act, Hare arrested over thirty suspected Kelly sympathisers. Without any evidence of wrongdoing, many suspects were detained from January to April, which, being harvest time, threatened the livelihood of many of the men, predominantly selectors and rural labourers. The detention was probably illegal, but magistrates were eager to wipe out the network of sympathisers who worked the 'bush telegraph'. Over-zealous policing, however, only promoted unrest and galvanised resistance.

As one of the detainees said in court, 'If the police don't let us go soon they are going to have more than the Kelly gang to fight.' Hare didn't budge. Instead he went further, announcing in July that suspected sympathisers would be refused selections. This turned many more Victorians against the police. Kelly sympathisers started wearing their chin straps under their noses as an open symbol of their rebellion. At the same time, Hare only threw men in prison, leaving the female sympathisers to provide supplies and assistance to the four outlaws.

To make matters worse, the police were hampered by infighting and petty jealousies. Aware of the difficulty of tracking the outlaws in the Strathbogie Ranges, the police recruited six Aboriginal trackers from Queensland in March 1879. Ned had a lot of respect for the men he called 'those six little black devils', but the police were too busy stabbing each other in the back to make good use of the trackers. After several uninspiring months, Superintendent Hare was replaced by Assistant Chief Commissioner Nicholson. Then, in June 1880, Hare took over again. So, to recap: first Nicholson was in charge, then Hare, then Nicholson again, and finally Hare had another go. The police looked more like they were playing musical chairs than pursuing Ned and his gang.

While Hare was in charge, he recruited as many informers as he could. His star informer was Joe Byrne's old buddy, Aaron Sherritt. It was obvious that Sherritt was keen to claim the £8000 reward. In early February 1879, Sherritt had told police there would be a raid on Goulburn in New South Wales. There was a raid in February, but the target turned out to be Jerilderie, not Goulburn.

The families of the outlaws quickly came to distrust Byrne's former friend. After learning that Sherritt was co-operating with the police, Joe Byrne's mother had disallowed the marriage of Sherritt and her daughter. Sherritt then tried to court Kate Kelly, but Kate's older sister Maggie wouldn't have it. The one-time friend of the outlaws had turned into a bitter enemy. He led the police into the Strathbogie Ranges, pointing out camps Ned had used, but they were always abandoned. Rumours started spreading that the gang had left the country for New Zealand or America.

Another rumour had it that, after keeping a low profile for sixteen months, the gang was about to launch a major raid. Some metal had been stolen from ploughs near Greta and locals thought the Kellys were responsible. Indeed they were, the gang reshaped the stolen metal into suits of armour. Very heavy armour at that. Ned's suit and helmet weighed 44 kilograms, thick and strong enough to withstand at a distance of 10 metres even the heavy bullets the police used.

The four outlaws had been planning their raid for months. By creating a diversion at Beechworth, Ned wanted to draw out the police from Benalla. At Glenrowan, where the Kellys had plenty of sympathisers, the gang would then derail the police train and, clad in armour, force the surrender of the police officers. Ned had supplied the sympathisers at Glenrowan with guns and the next step was for these sympathisers to take the police into the hills and keep them there under guard. Meanwhile, the four outlaws would ride to Benalla and rob the unprotected banks. Afterwards, the gang would release the police prisoners only if Mrs Kelly was released from prison in return

By this stage the outlaws were sure they'd been betrayed by Aaron Sherritt. They wanted blood. On Saturday, 26 June 1880, Dan Kelly and Joe Byrne sought out Anton Wicks, Sherritt's German neighbour near Beechworth. They handcuffed and threatened to kill Wicks unless he went with them to Sherritt's house. At 7 p.m., Wicks knocked on Sherritt's back door and called his friend's name. As soon as Sherritt appeared in the doorway, Joe Byrne shot him dead. Then Joe and Dan called Mrs Sherritt, telling her she would have to bury her husband, as 'we've shot him for being a traitor'.

This was the diversion Ned Kelly hoped would draw the police swiftly from Benalla. Joe and Dan knew there were four police stationed at Sherritt's hut and the bushrangers had expected the police to give chase. Joe and Dan fired into the hut, taunting the police, but the four constables refused to step out into the darkness. Eventually, Joe and Dan mounted and rode into the night, reaching Glenrowan at dawn. Instead of giving chase, however, the police had ducked for cover under Aaron Sherritt's bed, where they remained for hours. It was 1 p.m. Sunday before one of them finally reached Beechworth with news of Sherritt's murder.

Meanwhile, at Glenrowan, Ned Kelly forced a group of railway workers to remove a length of track, expecting the police train shortly to be charging through the town on its way to Beechworth from Benalla. As Sunday passed, however, there was no sign of the train.

The gang had taken control of the Glenrowan Inn, where they made merry as they kept watch over about thirty-five captives, including the local policeman. Another captive was schoolmaster Thomas Curnow, who befriended Ned. Curnow eventually asked if he could take his wife and return home. Ned agreed but said, 'Go quietly, and mind you don't dream too hard.'

Finally, long after midnight on Sunday night, Ned came to the conclusion that the police weren't coming. It was time to bail out of the plan. But, just as Ned was giving his regular valedictory account of how the Kellys had been persecuted and victimised, he heard a train whistle. 'By Christ, that bastard Curnow has tricked us,' Ned exclaimed. And indeed he had: at 3.25 a.m., Curnow had stopped the police train by waving a red handkerchief, letting the troopers know the gang were at Glenrowan and that the track had been deliberately damaged. Shortly afterwards, the local police officer, Constable Bracken, arrived, reporting that he had just escaped from the Glenrowan Inn, where the gang was holed up. The police had all the information they needed.

Hearing the whistle, Ned rode out to investigate. He saw there were two trains: a pilot, and a second train behind. Even if Curnow hadn't waved his red handkerchief, only the pilot would have been derailed. Among those on board the second train were Superintendent Hare, nine police, the six black Queensland trackers, five reporters and seventeen horses.

Ned returned to the inn and the outlaws wriggled into their cumbersome suits of armour. Meanwhile, the police were unloading their horses at Glenrowan station. The gang decided to attack. Exactly what happened next is uncertain. Hare claimed the outlaws fired first from the inn; Ned claimed it was only after the police had fired several volleys that the gang started shooting. Either way, a gunfight ensued. Ned was soon hit in the foot and the arm; Superintendent Hare was also wounded. Shortly afterwards, Joe Byrne was hit in his right calf.

Under heavy fire, Joe, Dan and Steve ventured out of the inn, only to be forced back inside by the spray of gunfire. The gang hadn't slept since Friday night and had been drinking steadily all Sunday, and suddenly they found themselves dodging bullets in their heavy armour. They were exhausted. Inside the inn was utter chaos. Besides the outlaws, thirty-five men, women and children were sprawled about the floor trying to avoid the bullets which were piercing the inn's insubstantial walls. There were screams and moans and mayhem, particularly after thirteen-year-old Johnny Jones (son of the licensee, Ann Jones) was fatally shot in the stomach. Johnny's sister Jane was hit in the head too. Several captives tried to escape. Some succeeded, but others were forced back inside by the police's incessant firing.

After ten minutes of fighting, two rockets were fired on the far side of the railway, the prearranged signal for the sympathisers to come and assist. There certainly were plenty of armed locals at hand—there had even been talk of forming a north-east republic—but it is impossible to know just how far the sympathisers were prepared to go to support Ned's gang. Given that the plan had miscarried, with the gang now under seige, the sympathisers held themselves back. Under these circumstances, they certainly weren't prepared to open fire on the police officers.

As the shooting continued, the wounded Superintendent Hare departed for Benalla before Superintendent Sadleir arrived to take command. More than a dozen police reinforcements arrived on the scene. Another group of civilians trapped in the inn made a desperate bid to escape. Mrs Reardon led the way, a baby in her arms and two children in tow. One of the police bullets passed through the baby's shawl; her nineteen-year-old son was hit in the shoulder. Screaming, the family of four just made it to safety.

At 5 a.m., through a gap in his armour, Joe Byrne was shot in the groin, apparently while drinking a glass of brandy in the bar. He died shortly afterwards. Then, mistakenly believing Steve and Dan were behind him, Ned rushed from the inn. The police didn't know who it was beneath the long grey overcoat and metal helmet. Ned advanced and fired wildly, managing somehow to advance beyond the police cordon. There he collapsed onto the ground, wounded and weak. With so many sympathisers so close at hand, Ned probably would have been able to escape; instead he took hold of his three revolvers and turned back towards the hotel, hoping to rescue Steve and Dan, now that he'd realised they hadn't made it out with him. 'Dogs, you can't shoot me,' Ned yelled. 'Come out boys, we'll whip the lot of them.'

The police (there were thirty-four of them now) fired relentlessly at this man who seemed indestructible. Hit again and again, Ned kept advancing. Constable Arthur aimed for the slit in the helmet, while, from close range, Sergeant Steele fired at his knees with a double-barrelled shotgun. His armour was hit seventeen times; his body suffered twenty-eight separate wounds. Finally, Ned Kelly toppled backwards. 'I'm done for,' he yelled. The police rushed forward and prised off the helmet, only then realising who they had captured. Sergeant Steele kicked the wounded bushranger in the groin and thrust his pistol in Ned's face. Constable Bracken stopped Steele pulling the trigger: 'You shoot him and I'll shoot you,' Bracken said. 'Take him alive.' The police lifted their prisoner and carried him to the railway station. Ned was near death.

Ned Kelly was captured and Joe Byrne was dead, but for hours the shootout with Steve Hart and Dan Kelly continued. Finally, in the afternoon, a silence descended. The police decided to set fire to the inn, forgetting that one wounded old man, Martin Cherry, was still inside. All the other innocent captives had escaped. At 3 p.m., Constable Charles Johnson rushed up to the inn with a bundle of straw which he then set alight. The straw blazed up, but soon died out. Like many local buildings, the Glenrowan Inn was made of fire-resistant stringy bark. At this point, one of the Kelly sisters, Mrs Skillian, rode up and asked whether she would be allowed to enter the Inn to convince Dan Kelly to surrender. Just as the police were deciding whether to let her, the building burst into flames, the calico and furnishings had caught fire.

With the flames spreading, a Catholic priest, Father Gibney, bravely advanced to the inn, holding a crucifix in front of him. Several

Sub-Inspector O'Connor and five of the black trackers who were brought down from Queensland to hunt the Kellys.

police followed. The men stepped inside, where they found the body of Joe Byrne in the bar and the bodies of Steve Hart and Dan Kelly in a small parlour beside the bar. Rather than surrender, Steve and Dan had turned their rifles on themselves.

Father Gibney and the police only had time to carry the slightly scorched body of Joe Byrne from the building before a gust of wind made the heat unbearable. They rushed outside, barely escaping before the Glenrowan Inn collapsed. Hours earlier a telegram had been sent to Melbourne requesting a cannon to blow down the house. Now, with the afternoon shadows lengthening, a second telegram was sent saying the cannon was no longer required. The 12-pounder Armstrong gun, already on its way, was stopped at Seymour. Martin Cherry was found in the detached kitchen behind the inn, but the old man died before nightfall.

After the fire died down, the unrecognisably charred remains of Dan Kelly and Steve Hart were pulled from the inn and given to Mrs Skillian for burial. Among the remains, the police also found two suits of armour similar to the one worn by Ned Kelly. The police held onto

EDWARD
(NED) KELLY

V. R.

£8000 REWARD

ROBBERY and MURDER.

WHEREAS EDWARD KELLY, DANIEL KELLY, STEPHEN HART and JOSEPH BYRNE have been declared OUTLAWS in the Colony of Victoria, and whereas warrants have been issued charging the aforesaid men with the WILFUL MURDER of MICHAEL SCANLON, Police Constable of the Colony of VICTORIA, and whereas the above named offenders are STILL at LARGE, and have recently committed divers felonies in the Colony of NEW SOUTH WALES; Now, therefore, I, SIR HERCULES GEORGE ROBERT ROBINSON, the GOVERNOR, do, by this, my proclamation issued with the advice of the Executive Council, hereby notify that a REWARD of £4,000 will be paid, three-fourths by the Government of NEW SOUTH WALES, and one-fourth by certain Banks trading in the Colony, for the apprehension of the above-named Four Offenders, or a reward of £1000 for the apprehension of any one of them; and that, in ADDITION to the above reward, a similar REWARD of £4000 has been offered by the Government of VICTORIA, and I further notify that the said REWARD will be equitably apportioned between any persons giving information which shall lead to the apprehension of the offenders and any members of the police force or other persons who may actually effect such apprehension or assist thereat.

(Signed) HENRY PARKES,
Colonial Secretary, New South Wales.

(Signed) BRYAN O'LOGHLEN,
Attorney General, Victoria.

Dated 15th February, 1879.

The gunfight between police and the Kelly gang at the Glenrowan Inn.

the body of Joe Byrne for an inquest, later stringing him up outside the Benalla police station for photos. Aware of the volatile atmosphere, of how many Kelly sympathisers there were ready to take up arms against them, the police hastily returned Byrne's body to his friends for burial.

Ned Kelly, the only survivor of the gang of four, made a remarkable recovery at Benalla. He said that the gang had known of all the police's movements. At Glenrowan, Ned said, the gang planned to spray the derailed train with bullets. 'But,' protested Inspector Sadleir, 'you would have killed all the people in the train.' 'Yes, of course,' replied Ned. 'They'd have got shot but wouldn't they have shot me if they could?'

After preliminary proceedings at Beechworth, Ned was tried in Melbourne for the murder of Constable Lonigan at Stringybark Creek two years earlier. The trial opened at the Central Criminal Court on 28 October 1880 before Justice Redmond Barry, the same judge who had sentenced Mrs Kelly to prison after the Fitzpatrick incident. There were no witnesses for the defence; and, under the law of the day, the accused was not allowed to give evidence on his own behalf. The following day, the jury found him guilty, after deliberating for only thirty minutes. With the verdict returned, Ned Kelly addressed the court:

> It's no use blaming anyone now … It is not that I fear death. I fear it as little as to drink a cup of tea. On the evidence that has been given, no juryman could have given any other verdict. That is my opinion. But, as I say, If I'd examined the witnesses, I'd have shown matters in a different light … For my own part, I don't care one straw about my life, nor for the result of the trial; and I know very

well from the stories I've been told, of how I am spoken of—that the public at large execrate my name … But I don't mind, for I'm the last that carries public favour or dreads the public frown. Let the hand of the law strike me down if it will; but I ask that my story be heard and considered.

Then he was sentenced to hang, whereupon Justice Barry said: 'I desire not to give you any further pain or aggravate the distressing feelings which you must be enduring … May the Lord have mercy on your soul.' Kelly replied: 'Yes, I will meet you there.'

A petition, signed by 60 000 Victorians, demanded that Ned's life be spared. On the eve of his hanging, a meeting convened to demand mercy was attended by 4000 sympathisers. There were similar meetings in Ballarat, Bendigo and Geelong, but to no avail. Also on the eve of his hanging, Ned was visited by his sisters Kate and Grace, his brother Jim (who had not joined Ned's gang because he had already been in jail at the time) and his mother, who was also being held prisoner in Melbourne Gaol. His mother told him to 'die like a Kelly'.

Just before 10 a.m. on 11 November 1880, Edward (Ned) Kelly, was led to the gallows. The *Argus* reported that his last words were: 'Ah well, I suppose it has come to this.' According to the *Age*, however, as the mask was put over his head, Ned declared: 'Such is life.' He was pronounced dead at 10.05 a.m. He was twenty-five years old.

Ninety people applied for a share of the £8000 reward. In the end, Superintendent Hare received £800 and handkerchief-waving schoolmaster Thomas Curnow received £550, while the four constables who hid under Aaron Sherritt's bed were even awarded £42 each.

Mrs Kelly was released in February 1881, returning to Greta, where she lived with her remaining son, Jim, and died in 1923, aged eighty-five. Jim, who remained a bachelor, died in 1945, aged eighty-seven. Until the end, both maintained a stoic silence about Ned and Dan Kelly.

A month after Ellen Kelly was released, in March 1881, a Royal Commission started investigating the conduct of the police during Ned Kelly's reign. In its wake, nearly every officer involved in the hunt was reduced in rank or dismissed. Hare and Nicholson were both forced to retire; three of the four constables who hid under Sherritt's bed were dismissed for cowardice (the fourth had already resigned); and Constable Fitzpatrick, the man who had started it all, would have been dismissed had he not already resigned. 'He associated with the lowest persons, could not be trusted out of sight and never did his duty', was the assessment of Fitzpatrick's superior officer.

As for Justice Redmond Barry, the man to whom Ned Kelly said, 'Yes, I will meet you there,' he didn't survive very long at all. Two days after Kelly was hanged, Barry collapsed, and ten days later he was dead. Such is life.

BIBLIOGRAPHY

The Australian Encyclopedia.
Boxall, George, *Australian Bushrangers, An Illustrated History,* Rigby, Sydney, 1975.
Dunstan, Keith, *Saint Ned, The Story of the Near Sanctification of an Australian Outlaw,* Methuen, Sydney, 1980.
Mendham, Roy, *The Dictionary of Australian Bushrangers,* The Hawthorn Press, Melbourne, 1975.
Nunn, Harry, *Bushrangers, A Pictorial History,* Lansdowne Press, Sydney, 1980.
Sharpe, Alan, *Bushranger Country,* Atrand Pty Ltd, Sydney, 1988.
Smith, Peter C., *Tracking Down the Bushrangers,* Kangaroo Press, Kenthurst, NSW, 1982.
White, Charles, *History of Australian Bushranging,* Volume 1, Lloyd O'Neil, Melbourne, 1970.
White, Charles, *History of Australian Bushranging,* Volume 2, Lloyd O'Neil, Melbourne, 1970.
Williams, Stephan, *A Ghost Called Thunderbolt,* Popinjay Publications, Canberra, 1987.

PICTURE CREDITS
Cooee: 1, 3, 22, 26, 27, 29, 31, *Murray David Collection:* 5, 9, 12 (left), 17, 20, 36 *Private Collections:* 10, 15, 21, 31
National Library of Australia: 4, 6, 7, 8, 10, 11, 12 (right), 17 (top, right), 22 (bottom, left), 24 (bottom, left),